TAKE IT EASY™

And More Tips for the Dedicated Improviser

"You've got to learn your instrument.
Then practice, practice, practice. And then when you
get up on the bandstand, forget all that and just play."
– Charlie Parker

TAKE IT EASY™: And More Tips for the Dedicated Improviser
By Ryan Millar
ISBN 978-90-827714-0-4
Copyright©2018 Ryan Millar
ALL RIGHTS RESERVED.
International copyright secured.

Printed in Ireland by Lettertec.

lettertec

Contents

PREFACE

This isn't an instruction manual. It's a collection of ruminations on improvisation. It's probably not the first book on improv you should read – it's maybe the fifth – but you should definitely read it.

Thanks to the tireless passion of improv devotees like me and you, and the discovery of new applications for the form, improv has grown from a fringe hobby enjoyed by few to a niche performance pursuit, and now into a position of respectability literally around the world. From weeklong festivals to full-time educational programmes, and in theatres and training centres, improv has well and truly arrived. (And that's not even touching on the application of improv in a business context.)

I've always been fascinated by both improv and the people it attracts. I love having a shared vocabulary with someone, a common currency, so that as soon as we meet, we know that we speak the same language and can have a bucketload of fun just by riffing off ideas and doing bits.

And though my individual capacity to talk about improv, teach workshops and classes and do shows is endless, I'm not currently in a position to travel to teach and perform nonstop. So I realised that putting all those ideas in one place was a much better way to go, some sort of repository for all the ideas I have and things I'd learned and discovered, which people could make use of if they chose. What I hit upon was a book. This book, to be precise.

Not that it'll stop me having hours of wonderful conversations about the craft I love – if anything, it'll hopefully increase my opportunities to talk about improv. But by writing it down, these thoughts can all be in one place. Plus writing helps me clarify, qualify and outline my ideas. And hopefully you'll get something out of it too.

So writing this book has been good for me, and hopefully reading it will be good for you. That's a win-win situation, which is one of my all-time favourite types of situations.

Improv and me

I took my first improv class while in acting school. At the time I thought I was going to be an actor, though I never really made an honest effort at pursuing that career. But I did take an eight-month independent-study acting programme at the now defunct Gastown Actors Studio in Vancouver. The certificate I received at the end of the course read 'Certificate of Acheivement. (Yes, 'achievement' was spelled wrong.)

I didn't notice the typo until proudly showing the certificate to my dad when he came to visit me in Vancouver one day. I still remember his expression as he did little, if anything, to mask his disappointment.

And fair enough, really – there were few real tangible positives that came out of that training. Of course, I did get some excellent acting lessons that serve me well in my occasional forays into the acting sphere, and obviously help with improv. But the biggest positive had a profound and lasting impact on my life – and that was my discovery of improvisation.

For it was here that I took my first improv class, and fell into it so hard that I've never fallen out of it. Now, nearly 20 years later, I regularly coach, teach and perform improv and comedy in and around Amsterdam, where I live, and at festivals and shows in other cities.

As I teach more workshops, I discover more what it is that I like, what I think students of improv need to learn and hear, and various other elements. In this time, particularly in the last few years, I've developed quite strong opinions about improv. Though there are many reasons to get into improv, and many ways it can be done well, I feel there are certain things that differentiate 'good improv' from 'beginner' – or 'accomplished' from 'wilfully terrible'.

As well as teaching and performing improv, I make part of my living as a writer, and the idea of putting these two pursuits together, and writing about improv, occurred to me. Then I couldn't shake it.

So I set to work taking all the things I've thought and discovered and picked up over the years, and shaping it into something that can be accessible to others, and hopefully useful for them too.

And here it is.

Ryan
December 2017

LEGENDS

- AllImprov – AllImprov does phenomenal work underpinning some of Amsterdam's most important and innovative improv groups and events. An early guarantee of support from them was instrumental in pushing me through some moments when I wasn't sure about carrying on. Solid!

- Jstar – From rooming together in Finland, doing a two-man Harold in France, to visiting a Hindu wedding in India, we've shared some times. And then this frickin' legend comes through with a major boost to my book project. Absolute legend!

- Chiara Ferracioli – Not just a wonderful wife and kick-ass mother, Chiara is also an ultra-supportive patron of the arts in general. And an ultra-patient supporter and booster of mine. I hope this book makes you proud. She's the best!

ACKNOWLEDGEMENTS

Firstly, Eva Carp for being a stellar designer and an unbeatable collaborator on this whole project. Noah Levin, Rod ben Zeev and Trent Pancy (Red Team) for their invaluable input in shaping and honing this manuscript. Intrepid proofreaders Nicola Tann and Simon Hodges for making the copy clean, and Noah Levin for helping me keep it that way. Guilherme Degasperi for the author photo on the cover. Stephen Sim, Tim Orr, Marshall Stern, Nancy Howland Walker, Jacob Banigan, Nicole Mischler and Trent Pancy for their excellent exercises I've included among the games and exercises in the 'Some Games to Play' section. And finally to all the players, participants, festival attendees, workshop participants, workshop leaders and teams and groups I've performed with or watched perform, thank you for all the inspiring conversations, questions, scenes and shows.

THE MOST IMPORTANT
THING IS TO BEGIN

1

INTRODUCTION

WHY TAKE IT EASY™?

I started teaching a workshop called TAKE IT EASY™ in 2012. As usual, the idea for the workshop came before the content. I'd noticed, when watching improv, that many people were trying too hard, and the result was uncomfortable, awkward and unfun scenes (for the players and the audience).

Furthermore, when people were in the flow and letting things happen, the scenes worked and everyone enjoyed them, from a comedic and an artistic point of view. But in discussions afterwards, people were often unsure how those wonderful moments had occurred and what they could do to ensure that they happened more often.

So I devised the TAKE IT EASY™ approach, to give them the tools to lighten up, have fun and allow the scenes to happen. Rather than digging at the walls of a scene like a prisoner armed with a spoon, looking desperately for an escape route, players could instead be like a black-belt martial artist in a botanical garden, enjoying the pleasant surroundings, keenly focused (and eminently watchable) yet prepared to spring into decisive action at a moment's notice.

> The exercises and ideas in here will give you more freedom onstage, help you be less attached to the outcome and more in the moment, and generally see you having more fun.

TAKE IT EASY™ isn't about a new way of doing improv, nor is it meant to replace your own style or approach. Instead it's a mindset that can inform your performance and your approach to improvisation. The exercises and ideas in here will give you more freedom onstage, help you be less attached to the outcome and more in the moment, and generally see you having more fun.

This is not an 'introduction to improv' book, nor is it a how-to manual. This book is a collection of thoughts and observations designed to give people a different perspective on their craft, and it also includes games and exercises for people to do on their own or to bring to their group to reinforce some of the principles and ideas and thoughts expressed herein.

NOTE: If you're wondering why there's a ™ after TAKE IT EASY, it's because I thought it would be fun to present this book like a comprehensive self-help programme and trademark it. Then I thought again, and realised that would be a whole lot of extra work, and just typing the title in all caps and putting the ™ symbol after it would probably suffice.

So that's what I ended up doing.

WHAT IS TAKE IT EASY™?

When we do something new and exciting, our body creates adrenaline, endorphins and other good hormones. When we perform in public and get a positive response, the feel-good hormones coursing through our veins increase. This is called 'good stress' and it allows us to improve performance. In job interviews, proposing to a long-term partner or running away from a bear, the extra boost of energy helps us.

But in stage performance, in improv particularly, that initial helpfulness is often offset by a type of sustained, low-level panic. We end up in a rush to do and say things, to respond to our partners quickly, to move onto the next things, to be loud, quick and excited. And we don't relax or reflect until we're offstage.

The problem here is that we miss out on a lot of what makes improv good (by 'good' I mean funny, engaging and connected). We also lose the ability to respond honestly and with conviction.

So, in our efforts to do something great, supported by our bodies endocrine system, we actually end up undermining ourselves. So what we need to do is slow down, take some deep breaths and approach the work a little differently. It will make improvising more enjoyable, and us more effective as players.

Imagine improv is a street fight. The antagonist loves a good brawl, is experienced in the bruising of knuckles, and is strong as a dump truck. His adversary is a nimble, hyper-aware martial artist, well-trained and poised.

If this were the movies, the martial artist would win every time – and maybe even in real life. But these two imaginary combatants aren't actually fighting one another. They're both you.

Except right now, you're the plodding dump truck. But with the TAKE IT EASY™ method described in this book, you'll start shifting towards the martial-artist mode. You'll develop the ability to move nimbly, let go of your ego and desire to win, and learn to better support your fellow players and scenes, and contribute more effortlessly to shows and workshops.

You'll also be able to make more use of your improv training and experience offstage too. It'll stop being confined to the weekly shows and trainings and permeate your regular life.

This book is laid out in sections. So you can read it cover to cover, or just dip into any section that catches your eye. It's my hope that you'll find lots of ideas here to inspire and challenge you, and that the exercises will be useful as you keep pushing yourself along on your journey[1].

---

1   If pushing yourself seems at odds with the idea of taking it easy, just remember that working hard is *always* a key to success. It's knowing what you need to be working hard at that can be a little tricky.

THE STRUCTURE OF THIS BOOK

This book has 10 different sections, each with a collection of essays. The most basic and fundamental concepts are near the beginning. Later chapters offer advice on dealing with frustrations, enriching your scenework, and so on. The next portion is an attempt to put your pursuit of improv into perspective, offering guidance about how to manage this activity in a sustainable and healthy way..

The last part is a collection of exercises – perfect to take with you if you're leading your group's rehearsal or teaching a workshop of your own.

This book is designed to be read from cover to cover, or to be picked up whenever you need a hit of inspiration – an idea for something to focus on for this afternoon's workshop or tomorrow night's show. Odds are, just by flipping through it and landing on a page, you'll find something to focus on.

I highly recommend that flip-and-find approach because by not planning and just seeing where you end up, there's a very good chance that the improv gods will smile upon you. It happens a lot – in fact it's one of the reasons you and I both love improv.

*YOU – JUST AS YOU ARE
– ARE MORE THAN ENOUGH*

2

GENERAL
STUFF

THE GOALS OF WHAT WE DO

"Don't judge each day by the harvest you reap but by the seeds you plant" – Robert Louis Stevenson

Individual improvisers have different reasons for doing what they do – to be funny, to express themselves, to take steps in a showbiz career, to come out of their shell, to meet people, or any number of other reasons. And it's not just that improv attracts a breadth of personalities – nobody stays static. People change, develop and grow over time. What caused a person to sign up to their first improv class may not be (and in fact, probably isn't) what keeps them coming back years later.

As for why a group of people do it, or what a specific group of players value artistically, it could be a lot of different things. Strong game of the scene, character or relationship journeys, detailed genre shows – all have their place.

Therefore talking about an improv goal for someone isn't that helpful, because we're all in it for our own reasons, and going in our own direction. And that's fine – improv is a broad church.

So when I say 'goal' it could actually be any number of things for you personally, or you might just like doing it, which is wonderful. And your group may have a completely different goal from the people performing before or after (or beside) you.

Let's leave those bigger aspirations aside then, and just think about your goals onstage when you're improvising.

Here they are:
- Have fun;
- Challenge yourself.

Both are important, but neither will sustain your work long-term on its own. If it's not fun, why bother? Of course you might get some harsh feedback in a workshop, have a bad show (or a run of bad shows) or have an interpersonal issue with a team member. Or whatever. If so, suck it up. Figure it out.

I doubt Mozart loved every moment of composing every note of his symphonies. I really don't think that, at the beginning of his career, Michael Phelps felt like getting up every morning to go swimming. But he did – at least often enough to own what seems like 200lbs of Olympic gold.

So if something gets you down, pick yourself up and get back into it. But if those rough patches or bad shows happen more often, or you find that you're not enjoying it, or there's something else that stokes your inner fire, don't be afraid to move on. Make some room in your life for something you enjoy doing, because it's important to have fun.

> If you're not challenging yourself then you're not growing as a performer, a comedian or a person.

But if you're reading this book, I imagine you're enjoying your improv, at least on some level, so that's good. But don't forget to challenge yourself.

If you're not challenging yourself then you're not growing as a performer, a comedian or a person. Lots of people enjoy doing stuff that doesn't challenge them (say, watching Star Wars again) or isn't good for them (say, eating an entire tub of Ben & Jerry's *Karamel Sutra* ice cream, for example). But eventually it gets boring.

A little bit of a challenge always helps us enjoy the moment and feel better afterwards. If you're getting too comfortable doing your regular shows with your regular crew, find ways to challenge yourself.

There's also a third goal – kick ass.

'Kicking ass' is the act of gliding through scenes with deft flashes of wit and inspired character choices; savouring the moments on the sideline as your teammates play their best; jumping in with delightful details and supportive moves just before they're needed; finding joy in everything onstage; and having the audience eating out of your hand.

If you've got a mix of these three things in your improv practice, you're doing great. If you're finding it hard to progress, or to consistently thrill and delight your audiences, or you've hit a rough patch, fret not.

These goals are exactly that: goals. The point of soccer is to score more goals than your opponent. But that doesn't mean every player kicks the ball towards the opposing team's net every time they get possession. They work towards that aim every chance they get by utilising all the tools, knowledge and fellow players they have, and assessing the situation as it changes. You can do likewise with your improv.

Your habits, thoughts and actions should be leading you toward these goals. And you should sometimes succeed and sometimes fail.

If you're bummed after a show, or don't feel like you're advancing, or otherwise things aren't clicking, don't worry. Instead just focus on the moments, and let your goals guide you. But don't let those goals take you out of the moment – this is improv after all.

LIVE IN THE NOW

> "Control of consciousness determines the quality of life."
> – Mihaly Csikszentmihalyi

Improvisers know it's all about 'the moment'. Much of the appeal of learning and practicing improvisation is the way it forces us to be completely present in the now. That presence – where we're not distracted by our inner monologue or checking social media on our phones – is powerful.

And it's something to revel in – from the moment we start warming up in a class or workshop to when we step onstage for a show. Being present is an addictive feeling.

However, after hundreds of hours of watching improv shows and teaching workshops, I began to notice something strange. Every few scenes (especially with beginners or young improvisers) a pair of improvisers will start talking about the future, looking ahead, as if they're trying to get to the next part of the scene.

It's as if the scene they're currently in is a preamble to something really good. As if whatever happens after it will be excellent and funny – they swear! – just please bear with them for the slow moments they're in now. The scene starts to falter. Their characters flatten, the dialogue gets stale, and desperate flop sweat starts to form.

Like Wile E Coyote looking down after he's run off a cliff, as soon as a player loses confidence in what's happening in the present, they plummet.

Like Wile E Coyote looking down after he's run off a cliff, as soon as a player loses confidence in what's happening in the present, they plummet.

The players start looking around for something to spice the scene up, start going faster or miss things, all to move past this mediocre present and get to the story. Not realising that the story itself is exactly where we are. Always. In the now.

The parallel that suggests itself to me now is someone intently searching through a house, turning the lights on, knocking people out of the way, declining the ice cold bottles of beer offered to them, looking under the bowls of potato chips on the coffee table, ignoring the attempts of their friends to get their attention.

Finally, they interrupt the DJ, who begrudgingly turns the music down. Then they ask her the question they've been trying to find the answer to: "Excuse me, I'm looking for a party. Have you seen one anywhere?"

And before the DJ answers, they rush off to another room, asking everyone to leave, so that they can find the party.

Your scene – whatever it is – is the party of the year. Don't miss it waiting for something that's about to happen, thinking about something that's already happened or talking about people who aren't here.

A SCENE IS A SCENE IS A SCENE

"If you always do what you've always done, you'll always get what you've always gotten." – Henry Ford

When I started improvising, it seemed the most common progression of an improviser was: start with shortform games in high-school drama or an 'intro to improv' class; if you like it, and get good at the games, you look for new challenges; sooner or later you discover the greater freedom of longforms like Harold, Montage or improvised plays (or whatever your particular fancy is); and then you turn your back on shortform.

It seems this trajectory is changing, and now, thanks to UCB and iO, longform is no longer something you get into *after* you learn shortform. Many people's first – and only – experience with improv is in longform.

It even seems that shortform is done less frequently than it used to be. Meanwhile, longform is thought of as more 'pure' or rewarding – a higher expression of the art. I also know some shortform players who disparage longform as slow and self-indulgent.

Neither side is wrong. But in the big picture, it's important to remember this – who fucking cares? Longform is fun and challenging and so is shortform. People who are outside the scene don't care about your silly rivalry, and you don't need to invest energy in it either.

I'm not suggesting you no longer have an opinion or preference, but I am saying that creating an artificial barrier between improvisers and improv forms isn't particularly helpful – for you or the craft.

If someone doesn't know billiards, they probably don't care about your explanation as to why 9-ball is way better than dumb old snooker, or that you think billiards is a more skilful game than bar-rules 8-ball. They just see you pushing coloured balls around a felt-covered table with your stick.

If you want to keep getting better at improv (and if you're holding this book, my guess is that you do), you should try some new things. If you've never done a set of shortform games, push yourself to try some, even just in rehearsal. And if you've never done longform because you just play short game-centric sets, shake it up.

SHORTFORM BOOT CAMP

When I moved to Amsterdam in 2003 as an exchange student, renowned comedy institution Boom Chicago was holding auditions. I signed up and went. Even though I felt like I tanked my audition, I didn't. In fact, I ended up landing a job as an actor on their corporate shows (and narrowly avoiding my other possible fate: working as a telemarketer. I'm not saying telemarketing is a bad job, but when compared with getting paid to perform improv, well, it sure *seems* bad).

Until I was hired there, I had spent most of my five or so years as an improviser (all of them) disparaging shortform – I was a *longform* improviser *thank you very much*! I probably even rolled my eyes when a well-meaning uncle or friend of a friend would use *Whose Line Is It Anyway* as a reference point in an attempt to understand what I did. I would then sanctimoniously explain to the unfortunate person why longform improv was far superior to that *stuff*. ("Snooker isn't 'real' pool....")

But as I started training in the Boom Chicago style, I learned that my laid-back approach to scenes wasn't going to work for their shortform corporate shows for non-native English speakers. I needed to get into a scene, establish specifics, wring as many laughs out of a scenario as possible, and deliver a killer finishing joke that brought on the blackout. Fast, loud, presentational, punchy.

Whether in a loose longform late-night set or a shortform corporate show, the dynamics of a scene are very similar. It's either successful or it isn't. It's either fun to play and watch, or it isn't.

Learning to perform that joke-powered shortform style permanently affected my play for the better. It made me funnier, more confident, more decisive, more commanding, and it's something I can use, no matter what type of show I'm doing – shortform or longform.

And that's something that's too often forgotten – shortform and longform are just different applications of the same skills. Or, as Gertrude Stein might say, a scene is a scene is a scene. Whether in a loose longform late-night set or a shortform corporate show, the dynamics of a scene are very similar. It's either successful or it isn't. It's either fun to play and watch, or it isn't.

3

FUNDAMENTALS

EASY LISTENING

"The most important thing I look for in a musician is whether he knows how to listen." – Duke Ellington

A good conversation is like a ping-pong match. The ball moves back and forth rapidly, with different spins and placement and strokes, but it's the same ball, and both players are fully engaged in the game, responding to what the other person has served them. A good conversation is similar – the game changes depending on what the other person does, and ideas go back and forth.

A good improv scene works the same way. Two (or more. Or fewer) players offering a back and forth of ideas and impulses, each guided by what the others are offering. It's so simple. And yet...

We've all had a conversation where you could tell the other person wasn't listening to you because they wanted to say something. Super-annoying. We've probably all also been that person at one point too.

And just like it happens in conversation, it can also happen onstage. We've all also seen improv scenes where other players try and drive a point of view, or particular idea.

I've sure been guilty of ignoring something my partner says because I was so sure that my hilarious idea was *soooo* much better. You've probably done the same. That's fine. We've all made mistakes.

And make no mistake about it – ignoring your partner *is* a mistake. There are three main problems with doing this.

- It makes you an asshole. Ignoring the things your partner says and does in a scene (just as in real life) is an asshole move. Granted, when this happens we're often not aware of it – we're just caught up in our own thoughts or have something we really want to say.

- The audience notices. Maybe not consciously, but part of their awareness catches these moments and their internal monologue says something like: "Didn't that person just say they're adopted? Why is the other one still talking about the costume party?"

- The actual scene – the one you and your partner should be building together – is having the oxygen and possibility choked out of it.

Here's the thing – your hilarious idea isn't real. Neither is the scene you and your partner are making up. The only real thing you have in a scene is the onstage connection between you and your partner. Cutting off that connection is a shortcut to unfulfilling improv.

The only real thing you have in a scene is the onstage connection between you and your partner.

But the opposite is also true – when players in a scene are keenly tuned into each other and taking on board and responding to the information, tone and gestures of the other, a fun free-flowing scene is the result. *Every*time. And to make it work, you don't have to do more – you just need to *be*. You need to TAKE IT EASY™.

LETTING GO

"When I play from my mind I get in trouble." – Stevie Ray Vaughan

There's often a moment before we let ourselves say or do something, a slight pause. It's the 'final check'. We use this to avoid embarrassment. This impulse to check what we say gets hardcoded in. This is evolutionary adaptation at work. Saying dumb, inappropriate or ill-thought-through things in a board meeting or at a party isn't helpful, but in improv, it's pure gold.

The thing is, when we assess our ideas as they come up, we start to necessarily slow down. Then, as we judge, we may start doubting our ideas. We may look for something funnier, smarter, 'better' or more original.

It may also happen with our partner's ideas. Maybe we think their idea isn't quite the great one that will really make this scene excellent, so we avoid committing, we wait, or demur, and hope something better presents itself.

> Commit yourself to what you and your scene partner are doing in the moment *in every moment* and the scene will be discovered. It will present itself.

And very quickly we're in a cycle of examining (or avoiding) ideas, until eventually, finally, some offer gains traction. The problem is that the longer you ignore – or evaluate and discard – the ideas presenting themselves, the more likely it is that what you land upon won't feel right, and the resulting scene will feel unfulfilling.

Listen to that scene

Here's where TAKE IT EASY™ comes in. Fuck all those questions and concerns. Be wholly uncritical. Commit yourself to what you and your scene partner are doing in the moment *in every moment* and the scene will be discovered. It will present itself. The scene will be what it wants to be, if you let it.

That's not to say there's only one possibility for what a scene could be – there are infinite shades and directions, but they all need to relate to, and be rooted in, the offers that have come before. Whichever direction you choose, based on what your scene partner is giving you, will take you somewhere cool.

The problem is the signs can be subtle. A simple hand gesture, a facial expression, a hesitation.... Anything could be the thread that will take you into the story. These offers can be hard to spot – especially if you're not paying attention. But if you are, you can just follow that idea, and the scene will unfold as if on its own. The difference between searching for an idea and following the natural thread is the difference between surfing on a wave, and splashing around in it – and possibly drowning.

LOVE YOUR MISTAKES

"The man who makes no mistakes does not usually make anything." – William Connor Magee

When I started improvising I messed up a lot. Everybody does when learning something new. At first that would frustrate me because I wanted to do it 'better' and not make any mistakes. But when I started understanding how mistakes work, and the good that can come from them – onstage at least – I changed. I got better by embracing my failures.

And I've also gotten better at applying those onstage insights to real life.

Improv mistakes

I took an improv workshop with Keith Johnstone once many years ago. One piece of advice he shared really stuck with me. He said: "Try, make mistakes, fail big and fail happily. If the audience sees you unbothered by your mistakes then they can enjoy them too, but if they see that you feel humiliated and ashamed, they will be uncomfortable."

And it works, generally. The audience loves mistakes when you do too. Whether it's walking into a scene at an awkward moment, failing at a game, or having a mobile phone ring in the audience, it doesn't matter what the issue is. The audience loves it if you deal with it confidently and comfortably. And by 'confident' I mean 'humbly and happily'.

And, perhaps paradoxically, they'll enjoy it even more than if your whole show runs smoothly and slickly. There's a very good reason for this.

When things don't go as planned, the tension ramps up – for performers and the audience. It is, all of a sudden, very real. They know you're not playing a stock character or idly bantering – now the intensity has heightened and everyone is sucked into the moment. Since improv is about being in the moment, this is exactly what you're going for.

The audience loves mistakes when you do too.

When something slips up, the autopilot switches off and everybody (should) focus on that mistake. Don't gloss over it. Explore it, find out why it happened and how it can help. There's lots of fun to be had in playing with those unexpected slip-ups, and lots of awkward disappointment in opting not to deal with them.

I've made lots of mistakes onstage and felt awkward and embarrassed, and then so did the audience. But when I've made mistakes myself and stepped into them, gloriously, all kinds of exciting and unexpected things have happened.

Once I was playing the shortform game Pearls On A String, where players come in one at a time with initially unrelated phrases the later players weave together. When it goes well, by the end of the piece a whole story has emerged from the various fragments.

On this occasion I decided that, rather than thinking how to play off the offers that had come before (which felt like 'planning'), I would just come on totally blank and say whatever popped out of my damn mouth.

As it turned out, my subconscious had latched onto the last thing I heard, and my contribution was basically repeating the idea my predecessor had come up with. It made no sense whatsoever and everyone onstage just turned and looked at me like "WTF?" This was in front of a crowd of 200 people at a raucous late-night Boom Chicago show. They also were super-confused. It ground the whole thing to a dead stop.

I was mortified, and unable to use that mortification for anything. And the game was doomed from that moment forward. Had I smacked my forehead and stepped back out of the line, or faked my own death, or just sat down and shook my head when it was my turn, or something, it could've become interesting. If I'd only acknowledged my screw-up gracefully, everyone could have had a laugh at my clown-ish expense, and onwards we go. But that's not what happened. Instead the exercise just limped to an awkward conclusion[2].

Here's a positive example. During a solo improv set I forgot the name of one of the characters I was speaking to, a guy who was running a marina. And so the character I was playing became the kind of yacht-owning jerk who didn't care about the names of people who worked for him. That screw-up led to the discovery that I was an asshole. The scene gained momentum and the characters more depth.

That's not to say that forgetting character names is a good idea – it's generally not – but any mistake can become fuel for the scene.

---

2   A colleague did valiantly attempt to make my screw-up part of the overall story. He just about succeeded.

TRYING TO BE FUNNY, TRYING TO BE *ANYTHING*

"The less effort, the faster and more powerful you will be."
– Bruce Lee

"Don't try to be funny!" is something improv teachers often tell beginners. There's a good reason for that (and it's not because your teacher prefers unfunny improv). It's that trying to be funny rarely – if ever – results in great comedy. I'm not talking about trying in the sense of dedicating yourself to your craft and honing your comedic voice. That's important, especially if you're studying improv as a way to advance a career in comedy.

But in the moment – especially as a beginner – spending time in your head trying to think up a funny thing (instead of just saying the thing you're already thinking of) is a bad way to go for a few reasons.

- It means you're thinking/planning instead of listening to your partner.
- It slows down your scene.
- It instils a habit of second-guessing yourself.
- It's rarely worth the effort, laugh-wise.

The most counterproductive thing is that people will freeze up because they think the thing they're going to say isn't funny, so they don't do anything. This doesn't help. At all. It slows the scene down and knocks the performers out of the present scene.

Having the mindset of 'I need to be funny', especially at the beginning of an improv journey, rarely, if ever, results in achieving that goal.

Having the mindset of "I need to be funny", especially at the beginning of an improv journey, rarely, if ever, results in achieving that goal. More often it acts as an obstacle standing between the students and good scenes filled with genuinely funny moments. If you trust yourself, and let go of the need to try and be funny, you'll be so much better off. The key is to let down your guard, abandon your expectations, and instead focus on being present at all times.

Once that happens, you'll actually find laughs arriving. Genuine responses will elicit positive audience feedback. And once this process is in place, you can then certainly start making the funny more funny.

By letting go of the trying, the pressure comes off, and you can focus on staying present and having fun. This is how finding the funny fits into the TAKE IT EASY™ ethos.

It's like a Zen koan: only through not being funny will you be able to find the real funny.

THE PROBLEM WITH 'YES, AND'

"I am convinced that life is 10% what happens to me and 90% of how I react to it." – Charles Swindoll

'Yes, and' is the piece of advice most easily – and frequently – dispensed about improv. The idea is that any line of dialogue or idea offered by any player is immediately accepted ('YES!'), and immediately built upon ('and…').

If a player says: "Hey Hal. It's a beautiful day for birdwatching." Their partner would not deny that offer ("We're actually at bakery making pretzels! Birdwatching? You're a crazy person!").

Instead, they would respond with something that accepts and builds on the birdwatching idea ("I need to see three more goldfinches to break my personal record." Or "after this can we go to the movies, dad?" Or "are you kidding me? It's like minus-eight out here!" All these notions accept the original idea, and add more information to help build the relationship and the world.

'Yes, and' binds improvisers together. (It's not just used onstage.) Plus, it's a useful shorthand to explain how improv works to the uninitiated and a tidy guiderail for early scenes (and indeed further down the line as well).

At a wedding in Texas a couple of years ago, I was speaking to a member of the bride's family who lived in New York. The woman asked me what I did and I told her "I'm an improviser".

She replied, "Yes, and...?"

It was one of the sharpest pieces of cocktail conversation I've ever been on the receiving end of. She showed she understood enough about my world to make a snappy joke, one that fit so deftly into the context of conversation that an untrained ear might not pick up on it. And (whether intentional or not) she reminded me very very *very* few people are 'just improvisers' – most of us either do it as a hobby or, if we do it professionally, we must do other things too, be it writing code, waiting tables, running a theatre, teaching improv, or making hats.

Because of all the wonderful things improv is (and it is most certainly many wonderful things) providing a stable income for grown-ass people to subsist on is not one of its strong points. But I digress (somewhat).

The issue here is that 'Yes, and' is often thought to mean adding things to a situation. While that's true, it's not the whole story – only applying part of the principle can lead to sloppy and uninteresting work.

For example, let's say a player says to another: "Hey Marjorie! I love your hair!" Marjorie (who now knows her name!) can respond with, "Thanks Jan. That Salvatore is a master!"

This creates agreement on the reality and the circumstances, and the scene can now move forward. This is a perfectly suitable illustration of 'Yes, and'.

However, if they continue 'Yes, anding', we can end up with something like the following:

- Hey Marjorie I like your hair
- Thanks Diane, it goes really well with my brand new dress
- Oh, you got a new dress for the Fireman's Ball tonight
- Yes, I hope Reggie is there
- He's so handsome, did you hear that he got a new tattoo of a dragon on his back!
- Oh my god, what a rebel! I hope he rides his motorbike!
- Motorbikes are so dangerous, my uncle broke his leg riding a motorbike in Morocco.

They could go on like this forever, never arriving at anything particularly interesting. It conforms to the letter of the law of 'Yes, and' but not the spirit. That's why absorbing info and responding is just as – if not more – important than 'Yes, and'.

The other pitfall of 'Yes, and' is that it can train us to never say 'no', and saying 'no' is totally fine. Marjorie for example, could feel that her hair doesn't, in fact, look good. That can add some character information and suggest some context for the relationship too.

Marjorie could respond: "Aw, you're just saying that – it looks like a dirty paintbrush." Now the scene goes in a different direction. Perhaps she's annoyed by Jan's fake compliments, or her neediness compels her to extract ever more elaborate compliments. Maybe she's just hacked it off with a bread knife because she needs to hide from the police.

The point is she doesn't need to automatically accept her friend's compliment. She just needs to respond in an honest way for her character, and *not* be in robotic 'Yes, and' mode. A character saying 'no' can add variation to your improv show, which (if used appropriately) can contrast all the general agreement quite nicely. It adds another layer to the cake, gives another note to the song.

But they don't yield very good results at the beginning of an improv journey. When I'm teaching absolute beginners, I tell them they can't ever say 'no'. There's a 'no nos' rule. This might seem harsh, but I don't care. I will shut a scene down for a 'no'. This is because early improv training is largely about getting used to agreement, to associating, to building realities in a collaborative way. Once we're used to doing this without thinking, we can play with other options. At the beginning a 'no' almost always comes as the easiest way to block another's ideas, and thus prevent anything happening that's outside the player's control. But outside the player's control is exactly where we want to be.

> 'Yes, and' is a device used to create a shared reality – it's not just a free association on the last thing your scene partner said.

The second place 'Yes, and' gets us into trouble is when we keep piling information into a scene, thinking we're 'Yes, anding' (well, technically we are!) but in actual fact we're just ploughing more information into a scene and bogging it down. The example scene above shows what can happen if this approach gets out of control.

Think of 'Yes, and' as the grease of a scene – you need the scene to be greased up to get the pistons moving, and the pistons need to keep firing, but if you keep piling more 'Yes, and' in, the works get all gummed up.

If you say 'Yes, and' in your mind, and then add in something tangentially related, you end up with a whole mess of empty promises to the audience.

'Yes, and' is a device used to create a shared reality – it's not just a free association on the last thing your scene partner said.

4

LEVELING UP

ON THE NOSE

"The world is full of obvious things, which nobody by any chance ever observes." – Sir Arthur Conan Doyle

Too often beginner improvisers start a scene with the suggestion 'carnival' with a line along the lines of: "Oh boy, here we are at the carnival!" Of course, it's generally new improvisers who work in this way, but even experienced improvisers can end up doing variations of this. If the suggestion is 'carnival', they may end up with an initiation like: "The carnival rules! Let's go on the bumper cars!"

It's not wrong, it just looks and feels like 'ticking a box'. And theatrically speaking, it's a little 'on the nose'.

'On the nose' is a term often used for scriptwriting when the dialogue deals too much with things the characters would be unlikely to comment on[3]. Like being at the carnival and saying: "Oh boy, here we are at the carnival."

I can't count the number of factory scenes I've witnessed where the opening line of dialogue is a variation on "here we are at a factory…". If you're really working at a factory, you surely never say anything like that! A line like this sacrifices the reality of the scene in order to satisfy a felt need that isn't real. There's no real benefit to this.

You wouldn't expect an office worker to lean back in his chair and comment to his colleague: "Hey Marv, this sure is an office job!" And then have his partner to agree: "Yes, we are at work!" It sounds dumb, unrealistic, and offers nothing other than reinforcing something that's already been established. It doesn't inspire the

---

3   'On the nose' could also be characters speaking something that is actually subtext (the emotion underneath their dialogue), like a husband telling his wife "You cheating on me really damaged my sense of manhood". Or a middle-schooler saying "Let's get back at the bully and score a victory for the underdog!"

players, the characters are doing something weird and phony for no good reason, and the audience is struggling to find something in the scene worth investing in. Even though the players think they're creating a scene, they're just digging themselves a hole.

Only by accepting the reality without comment can the players start to get a scene going. Think about your everyday life "when you're on the bus, or driving your car what do you think about, or talk about with friends? If you don't walk into a Starbucks and say: "Here I am at a Starbucks", what *do* you say? Those things that you actually say and do in those circumstances (or would say and do if you were on a pirate ship, in a parking garage, or on a distant moon), that's what gives you a starting point.

> Being less obvious, less 'on the nose', gives players the ability to open up scenes, relationships and directions that are more fruitful.

Someone at the carnival may very well say "let's go shoot water in a clown's mouth" or "this is sooooo much cotton candy!" or "this is so romantic". They may not comment on the carnival for a while, and then weave it in later in the scene (or not). The office workers may lament the new coffee beans in the break room coffee machine, or comment on their new co-worker, or talk about an upcoming deadline, but they probably wouldn't talk about the fact that they're at work.

Being less 'on the nose' gives players the ability to open up into fruitful scenes, relationships and directions. And do it right away, without plodding through weird distracting details. In the carnival example it's not the carnival itself that is interesting, it's how the estranged father and his eight-year-old son navigate the son's motion sickness, or how the high-school sweethearts address the fact that they're about to go to different colleges, or how the carnies simply watch the rubes go by and reflect on their own lack of retirement savings, or even a fixed address.

The carnival isn't the point – it's just the context, the launch pad. How these specific characters navigate this day in this world is what matters.

Nadine Antler from Hamburg calls the main action of the scene 'the cake'. And an improv scene, she says, is never about 'the cake'. The dynamic of the scene is about the characters. For example, in a scene about a woman visiting a mechanic to get her car fixed, the fixing of the car is 'the cake'. Focus on that action and your scene will feel stilted and lack drama. Delve into the interpersonal, the feelings each character has about the other and the situation, and you've got shedloads of dramatic possibility.

CHANGING THE GAME

"The essence of the beautiful is unity in variety."
– Felix Mendehlsson

A note I frequently give improvisers of all levels is this: have variety. Mix it up. This variety applies to every aspect of what you do: characters, how you start your scenes, the games you play in your shortform set, the length of your scenes, the staging of scenes. But most importantly: the energy. There's a big difference between having a house style and being repetitive (or 'samey').

Audiences tire of seeing the same thing over and over again – even very fast-paced funny shows need variations. Different characters, slower reveals, musical interludes. Fast scenes followed by slower more patient scenes. As a parallel, think of Bohemian Rhapsody. Queen's operatic Prog Rock epic.

Think of the internal changes that make it memorable. Think of the beginning line "Is this the real life? Is this just fantasy?" Then think about the crazy guitar solo before it gets into the plinky "Scaramouche Scaramouche", the falsetto "Galileo", the sweeping chorus who reflect the lyrics back, that bitchin' guitar part....

It has all those big style changes and variations, yet it all fits together as a single song; a cohesive artistic unit. Of course, Bohemian Rhapsody lies at an extreme end of the 'style shift' spectrum, but almost any song you can think of contains plenty of variation. Those changes are part of what draw us to it – the chord progressions, the key changes, the bridge, intros and outros, lyrical themes, etc.

Now think of an album you like. The sound of the band doesn't change, but the songs do. They have different tempos, different themes, but they all fit into one overarching recognisable style.

A scene is like a song, and a show like an album. I'll say it again: A scene is like a song and a show like an album.

During a show, there should be some variations within your scenes. And from scene to scene there can be some similarity in tone and style (not to mention characters and subject matter), but there should also be some differences.

There's an improv tendency to follow one scene with another of a similar energy or content, which is only logical – if you're paying close attention to a scene (and of course you are), you might come out to start the next scene with a similar energy to, or an idea from, the previous scene. This is subconscious. And much of learning to TAKE IT EASY™ is empowering our subconscious to do the work.

But it doesn't mean you should be on autopilot. A good improviser finds different ways to both go with the flow and put their paddle in to steer a show in different directions.

Think of a scene like a song, and a show like an album. There should be some variations within your scenes, but there should especially be variations between your scenes.

If a high-energy big group musical scene finishes to a rapturous applause, you're going to have a hard time matching or topping that energy. But if you came on slowly and in silence, sat down cross-legged on the floor and sighed loudly, the energy has totally changed. What's going to happen in this scene? I don't know!

But I do know I'm not comparing it to the musical scene that came before.

And vice-versa. If there's a slow, patient, grounded, relationship scene, you may feel inclined to come on and match that energy. But a chef isn't going to follow a delicate creamed vegetable soup with a main of delicate creamed veggies. Nope. She's trying to create a different texture and taste that will complement what came before, not imitate it. You should do likewise. To create a complete experience, it's vital you pull a few different tricks out of your bag.

Album-wise, you would want to include a variety of songs that all fit a certain artistic ideal. Not just a bunch of stuff that sounds the same.

Seeking this variety may feel risky, but humans are predisposed to crave variety. We may have a favourite food, but that doesn't mean we want to eat that food all the time. And we love our favourite band, but that's not the only music we listen to.

It's the same with improv – we want some variety. This isn't just for within shows – it also goes for across shows as well. You don't want to play the same character each time you step onto the stage, or have your troupe rely on the same set list or form each time you perform. You need to give yourself the space to play in new ways, even as you develop a consistent voice as a player and as a group.

This diversity, though it may seem antithetical to the TAKE IT EASY™ approach, is actually a perfectly natural response to our innate human desire for some variety in our lives.

For shortform, this means the games you play should use different mechanics and flex a variety of muscles between scenic, musical, panel, story, genre and group games. Part of this is of course down to whoever is designing the set list, but a big part of that responsibility rests with the players.

And if you're doing longform, be aware of the energy in your scenes, and how to best support the overall show by slipping in a different vibe (via a faster pace, a bigger character, a shorter scene, a tender moment...) when required. You're creating an album, so you'll need to change things up now and then.

Plus, in trying new things, taking risks and playing with structure, you create new patterns and rhythms, continuing the artistic evolution of you and your group.

So be true to yourself, your style, and your group. Just don't get caught in a rut.

TOO MANY TOYS

"The main thing is to keep the main thing the main thing."
- Stephen Covey

When we were kids, if we were lucky we had lots of toys. And we used to love playing with them. Now that I have a daughter, I notice something similar – she loves getting toys and has been quite spoiled by friends and family on this front. But she can only play with one at a time.

Sure you could make the GI Joes go to Barbie's Dream Castle, or stuff your Lego into your Millennium Falcon. But still, you can't do that and play with the Rubik's Cube *and* the hula-hoop. (I feel like these toy references are dating me, but I grew up in the Eighties. That's just a fact.)

Anyway, this 'too many toys' idea lines up exactly with improv. When we 'Yes, and' too much, we end up with an unwieldy situation and confused players.

Two characters having lunch at a golf-course clubhouse might start chatting about one's husband's suspected cheating, the other's recent promotion, their high-school rivalry, a golf tournament that's happening today, the overcooked steak, and so forth.

It's not that any of these aren't good – they all have story potential. But that's precisely the problem – which one is *the* story? We may never know. And as soon as one becomes the focus of the scene, all these other elements get abandoned. This byproduct is also unsatisfying.

It works similarly with characters. If you try to detail a character too richly, (an opera-loving elderly tennis enthusiast with an English accent who loves sushi, and used to be a property lawyer who never learned how to drive, for example), you may find it's tough to give all of these elements the attention they deserve. Like a child who can't choose between a plastic sword and a bag of marbles. But if you and your partner agree and play with that toy together (and see what results from focusing on that), you're on the road to Funtime.

Character-wise, that might look like choosing just one or two attributes to play, and scene-wise that means going with what inspires you first, rather than generating more material than you can possibly use.

Remember, you only need one toy at a time.

DEEP INTO THE DETAILS

"Caress the detail, the divine detail" – Vladimir Nabokov

Treated with care, an offhand, almost neutral, opening line such as "You look nice today" can be turned into a juicy gateway to a rich situation. By being a little more patient, and adding some detail, you can create some more energy and information for your partner to work with.

Eleven quick options to turn that neutral offer into a detailed one

- "You look nice today. That red dress really looks great with that lipstick."
- "You look nice today. They'd be fools not to hire you."
- "You look nice today. Blue is really your colour."
- "You look nice today I guess *you* slept alright!"
- "You look nice today. Those glasses really suit you."
- "You look nice *today*."
- "You look nice today, but a court date isn't just about a sharp suit."
- "You look nice today. I love what you've done with your hair."
- "You look nice today" (with air quotes around the word nice)
- "You look nice today. If you'd have asked me out looking like *this* I'd have said yes for sure."
- "You... oh wow. [Pause. Rubs eyes.] You look, uh... nice today."

By giving our offers a little more definition, we remove the need for them to think of something new, or for our scene partner to do anything more than just be affected by the line, and unpack it.

They only need to take the first association they have, based on their life experience, whatever else has happened in the show up until this point (maybe they're dressed up for an awards ceremony, or have a second date this evening, or are doing their very first drag show, or...) and that, combined with the rich opening line, gives us a whole bunch more information about the context, the characters and where this scene might be going.

Compare that world of opportunity with the amount of work they would need to do off the back of "You look nice today". It's worlds apart. And it's not just this example. All too often a quick instinctive line would benefit from being pushed just a little bit further. Adding a bit more detail requires paying more attention to everything we (and our partners) do, but the rewards are worth it.

Details are challenging

Increasing our attention to every moment takes some getting used to, but it pays immediate dividends. It's impossible to be disengaged when enriching your scene with important details and making each moment matter. There are only things to be gained.

> It's impossible to be disengaged when enriching your scene with important details and making each moment matter.

One exercise I created (which I share in the exercise section of this book) is called the Roadshow. It involves partners collaboratively describing an imaginary object. What happens when two people are completely focused on finding details is that all elements of a scene present themselves, without any effort needing to be expended.

Objects become real, and relationships, history, and story are established as a byproduct, even though I've expressly set up the exercise as being only about the object. For details, the lesson is pay attention to them, because the story lies in those details. If you gloss over them, you risk leaving the story and scene covered up.

TWIST, DON'T BREAK

"In the theater the audience wants to be surprised – but by things that they expect." – Tristan Bernard

Audiences love to be surprised. That's how comedy works – the punchline is a surprise. Stories work this way as well – a plot twist creates more intrigue, and draws a viewer/reader deeper into the story. A predictable or formulaic story (or telegraphed punchline) robs the audience of that 'aha!' moment, and creates unsatisfactory entertainment.

And I absolutely do not suggest you aim for anything less than satisfactory entertainment (in fact, you should probably aim even higher than that). But in the desire to surprise the audience and our scene partners, in a rush to be seen as inventive or clever, we can lose sight of a very important (though less well-known) fact.

Audiences love to be surprised, yes. But just as much, they love to be *un*surprised. While a good plot twist or witty *bon mot* can thrill and delight an audience, so can stating the obvious, or doing the expected. Too many plot twists, or a succession of non sequiturs can throw an audience off.

In an attempt to be witty or surprising, players can end up saying and doing nonsensical things. Sometimes, the things we think will have the audience marvel at our cleverness has them rolling their eyes at our transparent neediness.

Take this example:
- Captain, we need your help with this.
- Ah, finally my black belt in ancient Kung Fu will come in handy!

OK. Sure. That's unexpected. It offers a direction for the scene to go, and even adds depth to the character. But that player is definitely not taking it easy. Not at all. And the scene is going to be more work, for players and audience, as a result. I'm not saying that direction couldn't work, but why make it more difficult, just for the sake of the unexpected?

Why not just find out what help is needed? Or draw on your captain's training, in the first instance? Following the expected, what has been laid out, offers less resistance and (quite possibly) more rewards.

In the right hands simplicity can be a powerful tool.

Whether in individual lines, or trying to make sense of a bunch of disparate threads in a longform set, we can sometimes try to do too much work to bring them together. Or if they fit too neatly together already, we may try to spread them out, throw in some red herrings, abandon an already-established pattern or otherwise try to mess with what's been created.

It's fun to blow things up, subvert expectations, play against the direction and see what comes up. Sometimes, sure. But that's not necessarily better than just working with what's in front of you. When you TAKE IT EASY™, you roll with what comes. In the right hands, that simplicity can be a powerful tool.

I've seen funny and surprising lines and moves met with audience indifference. And I've seen obvious ones met with applause breaks.

Let's take a scene between two men at a bar at closing time. One player confesses to a murder. The other player, recognising this as a chance to also make a surprising revelation (and perhaps follow the pattern) says that he saw some aliens.

Sounds terrible, doesn't it?

However, rewind the same scene. Have the first player reveal they murdered someone, and have the second player laugh awkwardly and make excuses to get out of that bar as fast as possible. The first player quietly gets up and follows them out.

Which is more 'surprising'? The first.

But which makes for a more interesting scenario? The second, obviously.

Not in spite of being simple, but *because* it's simple, it goes from A to B. The story builds on what's come before. No major thinking, no curveballs. An expectation is set up, and then delivered upon. That's all you need to do.

Remember that if you're trying to think up clever things, you may be missing out on doing the one thing that everyone is actually excited about. All that work for nothing. Expectations set up and abandoned.

Certainly not everyone agrees, and this advice doesn't apply in all cases – of course curveballs and tangents have their place. But remember that trying to make the story as strange and surprising as possible can result in throwing in one too many kinks, and then the hose doesn't work anymore.

PRACTICE YOUR PRACTICE

"Practice and opportunity very soon teach the language of art." – William Blake

While living in London there was a stretch of years during which I didn't take any improv workshops. I'd been doing improv for a decade and a half at that point, and I knew my way around it pretty well. It was also before the explosion of improv activity in London, and I wasn't teaching either. Just performing a few times a month.

I began to notice that the risk, discovery, and joy began to seep out of my work onstage. My performances suffered from what I now recognise as stagnation. It's not that performances became joyless, but I found myself enjoying them, and the idea of improv, less. Fortunately, I managed to get on track – all it took was to get back to teaching and taking some workshops.

The workshop space is an important part of any practice. It's where we're encouraged to make mistakes, work with new ideas, and play with new people.

Of course, elements introduced in the workshop – be they in an approach to character, story, genre, scene mechanics, or anything else – may not make it into the next show you do, but they shift your boundaries, reinforce or challenge what you already know and influence your process. And once they're part of your process they will eventually find their way into your product. Even if you reject the ideas from the workshop, you've learned something more about how you approach the work.

For example, maybe iambic pentameter from an afternoon's Improvised Shakespeare workshop won't become part of your show that night. But if you do play a Shakespeare scene you will be able to put some of your learning into action.

> The practice of anything has positive ripples beyond their intended use

In addition – and this is unavoidable – you'll have a heightened awareness of the rhythms of language. Maybe your turns of phrase will become more considered, more poetic. Like morning sun glistening on a dewy rose blossom. Or something like that.

And that awareness of language will also have effects beyond your stage-self, because the practice of anything has positive ripples beyond their intended use. It's impossible to stagnate when we're constantly being challenged. I have an appropriate example.

Towards the end of my period of improv listlessness, I began training in London at Master Chang's Hapkido Academy, earning my green belt before I moved to Amsterdam. What Hapkido instilled in me – besides discipline, flexibility and a ferocious neck attack – was a renewed love for practice and study.

I loved the trainings, going twice a week almost without fail until I moved. Through that practice I rediscovered the joy of learning. And without making a conscious choice, I stopped neglecting my improv, and I started studying and teaching more.

And just as my martial arts training led to my choice to reinvest in my improv, so the content of an improv workshop will influence not just your performances – it will also seep into your real life. The process also works the other way – if you spend your outside-of-improv time being lazy or bitter or locked in a negative mindset, that will inescapably seep into your performances. Even worse, it will probably affect the dynamics of your group.

Even if you don't do anything negative, and you just stick with your regular life, normal habits and routines, and regular rehearsals with your group, the buzz will lessen and things will eventually stagnate.

The good news is that if you spend even a little bit of your offstage life trying new things that scare you, challenging yourself, and expressing dedication to what's important in your life, that will have a positive effect on your performances.

You'll also enjoy your life more, because you'll be doing cool things and meeting interesting people. It radiates outward to improve the rest of your life, just as it does when you're onstage to improve your performances.

ENJOY YOURSELF – THIS IS SUPPOSED TO BE FUN

5

MIDDLE PART

DO SOME OTHER STUFF

"If you're going to make connections which are innovative, you have to not have the same bag of experience as everyone else does." – Steve Jobs

You're killing it at improvisation. You've found your tribe, you're developing as a person and you're starting to deepen your dedication. You even bought this obscure book on improvisation, so you must be *really* into it.

Hopefully this book is providing you with some insights, thoughts and frames for becoming a better improviser, and if you've been reading it for a while, hopefully you've been applying these insights and sharing them with your group and all is trundling along smoothly.

You feel reinvigorated. You've moved past the plateau and are climbing again, and you're connecting better with ideas, feeling more grounded... In short, improv is awesome again. What's next?

Go do something else.

That's right: something else entirely. You owe it to yourself, and to your improv.

Improvisation draws on a wide range of sources – in fact it draws on anything that might be out and around in your brain and bag of experiences. If you grew up riding horses, collecting comics or getting into fights, you can bring that to your scenework and shows.

It also holds true for now. If you work at Starbucks or Goldman Sachs, or are a graphic designer, all of those things can be part of your improv. And should be. Because we bring what we have offstage into our onstage life.

And that's why you should get an offstage life if you don't have one. Now that you have improv it's easy to make it the focus of your life. Cool. That's a great idea. But remember that every little thing you do can become part of your improv life, whether it's a precise character choice based on a diving instructor you once had, or an anecdote from visiting an estranged cousin, or adding detail to a film noir scene based on your extensive knowledge of Raymond Chandler novels.

Here are a few things you can do to expand your range of experience and give you more fuel for your improv.

- **Take a trip somewhere – anywhere.** Whether a three-month backpacking trip to Southeast Asia, or an afternoon at the petting zoo, real-life trips offer new sensory experience, the chance to meet new people, and the chance for stuff to actually happen to you. And stuff for you to do – stuff that's outside your regular habits and routines.

- **Learn something new.** Take a sushi-making class, or an eight-week Spanish course, or learn to tie flies for fly-fishing or how to resole shoes – anything at all.

- **Write.** Writing is so useful. No matter what you do or plan to do. Whether you consider yourself a writer or not, you, as an improviser, write scenes when you're performing, so spend a little bit of time writing to help you improve this.

- **Watch movies.** You probably do anyway, but watch more, watch widely, and of course watch your favourite genre as well. Just watch as many as you can, and watch them again. Watch critically. Then discuss them.

- **Breathe.** It seems obvious, but breathing matters, and much more so than we tend to give it credit for – in fact, we tend to take it for granted. Take a moment and have a couple big breaths. See? You already feel better.

- **Meditate.** This is one of the best ways to improve everything
  you do. Just sit quietly for a while and try not to think about
  anything. Of course your mind will think about stuff, but
  just remind yourself to breathe, and try to let the thoughts
  drift away. It's hard not to think, and to just be – a sure sign
  that we need more calm in our lives.

6

COMMITMENT

COMMITMENT IS A SHORTCUT TO SUCCESS

"The moment one definitely commits oneself, then Providence moves too." – William Hutchison Murray

If you're a basketball fan and you go to a game, you're expecting to see players executing their crispest dribbles, shooting their most calculated shots and playing their most tenacious defence. I'm not even a basketball fan, but I know at a basketball game I'd want to see people trying their hardest to do their best. Whether they're professional or amateur is irrelevant – if they're not trying, I'll be disappointed.

On the other hand, I was recently walking through my neighbourhood and I saw a bunch of kids around seven or eight years old playing football and I was transfixed. They were pretty good, but they were so committed – lunging for every ball, diving to make saves, cheering each goal like it was a Champion's League Final. I couldn't stop watching.

> The greats make things looks easy, effortless even. But that doesn't mean they aren't committed.

And just as it is for the sports analogies above, so it is for improv – and music, movies, opera, paintings, sculpture, computers, carpentry… anything. You don't want to see a master carpenter's wobbly coffee table, or go to a concert where the band decides to play, like the first half of a few songs and the bass player doesn't bother plugging in her bass. And you won't buy an album or watch a movie that doesn't show 100% commitment to the finished product.

It's not just trying, though. The greats make things looks easy – effortless, even. But that doesn't mean they aren't committed. In fact, all of this goes double for the really talented – the virtuoso musicians, the preternatural goal-scorers, the innate comedian. If they're not committed to what they're doing, it's not just a shame – it's a tragedy of squandered potential.

Think of any person at the top of their field, and ask yourself if they got there with half-assed attempts. Nope. And even though you may not want to be a professional improviser, that doesn't mean you shouldn't treat it with respect – especially if it's something you care about. If you're just improvising for fun, then commit fully to that, and have the most fun you possibly can.

And for those of us who don't have all that raw talent? We've got little but our commitment to contribute.

COMMIT TO YOUR SCENARIO

"Do or do not. There is no try." – Yoda

Too much improv is never given a chance to succeed because we see timid or uncommitted players (not timid characters, timid players). If your character is chopping firewood, your best, simplest and strongest choice is to just get in there and chop firewood like your life depends on it. Like it really matters.

Hell, your character's life could depend on it. For all you know their plane may have crashed into a frozen mountain, and chopping this wood and lighting the fire could be the key to survival. Or they could be chopping wood to stoke the potbellied stove at a rented cabin where they've come for a romantic retreat. The stakes are different, but the commitment is unerring.

"Hey!" (I hear you cry). What if I want to half-commit, what if my character is half-heartedly chopping firewood because they're a resentful teenager (for example)? No problem. Just go at it 100% *completely* half-assed.

Some schools of thought hold that the character should be worn lightly over the improviser, or the whole scene should be played as if winking at your audience as you do these things. I don't agree. I'd rather see a player commit 100% to what they're doing, rather than 'pretending', or doing everything in 'quotes'.

An audience wants to believe, and willingly suspends their disbelief. There is zero danger of the audience thinking you've actually crash-landed in the woods, and you're mime-chopping firewood to really save your life. They want to see you invested so they too can invest in what's happening.

In my younger playing days I had two modes onstage – one being a full (probably intensely, and possibly occasionally terrifying) commitment and high-energy. The other was a laid-backed feigned indifference, basically telling the audience that I was so super-casual I didn't really care what they thought.

The mode of over-exuberance is the most embarrassing to me now, but also the one I respect the most. The projected attitude of nonchalance or indifference I regret completely.

This attitude did two things for me – it insulated me against any criticism or negative reactions, so there was zero risk and little chance for growth. The other thing it did was allow me to hide from the audience. I could do jokes and characters without actually presenting myself. I was keeping myself safe, by hiding from them. But, if they couldn't touch me, how could I possibly think that I would be able to touch them?

Dig deeper and work harder. Perform more often and more completely. More authentically. With unswerving commitment, intensity and drive.

It may seem counter to the TAKE IT EASY™ ethos, but it's not. TAKE IT EASY™ is about doing less in a more productive way. Deep commitment allows you to achieve this.

SHOW YOUR AUDIENCE A GOOD TIME

"The audience is the true mirror." – Yoshi Oida

Audiences come to a show to enjoy themselves, which they can only do when they feel like they're in safe hands. This is because the audience will unconsciously mirror your attitude and behaviour. This is particularly important when opening and closing a show, but also goes for all your side-stage and backline behaviour. It should go without saying that this has nothing to do with character choices, but everything to do with how you, as a performer, approach your time facing the audience when you're not in character or in a scene.

If you went bungee jumping and the guy tying your rope was shifting nervously and told you "Uh, I'm not so sure about this. I mean, I'm not really so good at tying knots. I like it, but it's just something I do for fun…" and then shrugged while not making eye contact with you. How would you feel?

Would you still go bungee jumping?

Obviously, watching an improv show isn't as life-threatening as jumping off a railroad trestle with a big rubber band tied around your ankles, but they're different manifestations of the same principle – for the audience to feel relaxed, they need to feel the leader is in charge. And, if you're hosting a show, you're the leader. If you're not hosting the show, but are performing in it, you're not a leader in the same way, but you're still more of a leader than someone sitting in the audience, and they need to feel like you know what you're doing. Your comfort and enjoyment will lead to their comfort and enjoyment.

Any music act that sells out a stadium knows that it's not just about playing the music – it's about putting on a show. Obviously, performing improv comedy in a room above a pub to a crowd of

15 or so friends (and friends of friends), is on a much different level than a sell-out stadium tour. But that's actually when it's most important.

I imagine that performing in a stadium to thousands of adoring fans screaming is, if not exactly easy, then at least facilitated by the fact that people are excited to see you; they want to be there, and they paid money to do so. In improv, none of this is necessarily true.

Act confident. Be grateful but humbled by the attention of the audience who did come. Double down on your commitment to having fun and doing a great show.

Which makes it all the more important to make them feel like they're investing their time well. If you suggest you don't want to be there, or the audience numbers are lower than you feel you deserve, or whatever, the show's chances of success start decreasing. You can just as easily turn it around, so that the chances of success start *in*creasing.

Think back to that bungee technician (bungee guide? Bungee master? Bungenie?), and how he or she might help someone loosen up and enjoy themselves. Act confident. Be grateful but humbled by the attention of the audience who did come. Double down on your commitment to having fun and doing a great show. All other things being equal, that should be enough.

In his seminal book *How To Make Friends And Influence People*, Dale Carnegie talks about the magician Thurston the Great, one of the biggest magicians of the first half of the 20th century. This is what Carnegie had to say on how the great magician became so successful.

"…Thurston had a genuine interest in people. He told me that many magicians would look at the audience and say to themselves: 'Well, there is a bunch of suckers out there, a bunch of hicks; I'll fool them all right.' But Thurston's method was totally different. He told me that every time he went onstage he said to himself: 'I am grateful because these people come to see me. They make it possible for me to make my living in a most agreeable way. I'm going to give them the best I possibly can.'"

It's an unabashed gratitude and enthusiasm that might seem a little out of place in our modern era, but that doesn't make it any less powerful. Nor any less appropriate.

Of course, you probably don't make your living as an improviser (if you do, congratulations! The dream is real!). But regardless, be grateful to your audience for coming and give them a show they can enjoy. To the best of your ability. Every time.

Clip-n-save commitment list

Listen HARD
Focus COMPLETELY
Concentrate INTENSELY
Care A LOT
Have Fun BECAUSE IT IS
Relax YOU DESERVE IT

WHEN YOU'RE INTERESTED,
YOU'RE INTERESTING

7

BE
YOURSELF

YIKES, THAT SHOW WAS BAD!

"Audacity, more audacity, and always audacity!" – Georges Jacques Danton

When I have a bad show, it bothers me long after I've left the stage. Of course I also remember some of the good sets – the times that kismet has smiled down upon me and my fellow performers, anointing us with the 'genius stick' as we've flowed from laugh to gasp and back to laugh, through a series of interconnected moments of sublime perfection. That warm glow lasts a while. But the stink of a bad show lasts much longer.

This is due to something called the 'negativity bias' or 'negativity effect'. Negativity bias asserts that we remember negative experiences much more easily than positive ones, or mentally assign negative experiences more weight than positive ones. So you can recall those missed flights, workplace disappointments and fights with your partner much more easily than you can call to mind the thousand little wonderful moments of your daily life. And the iffy shows and our embarrassing onstage miscues spring to mind more easily than those nights we were actually pretty good.

Many years ago, while I was living in Rome, I went back to Vancouver to visit. Shortly after arriving I guested with my friends at the Sunday Service and had a lights-out show. It was a triumphal return! Then, before I flew back to Rome a few weeks later, I sat in with them again. I did it even though I was hungover, tired and had plans to watch a hockey game. Bad call. It was awful. Or more specifically: I was awful. Awkward, slow-witted, uninspired. The antithesis of the show just a couple weeks earlier. The worst part is, thanks to the negativity bias, I generally don't even recall that first glorious wonderful show, just the awful one a few weeks later[4]. Thanks a lot, negativity bias!

---

4   In fact, I'd totally forgotten about the super fun show until writing this.

Some performers claim that the moment they walk offstage that last set – good or bad – is gone. I'm a little bit jealous of them, but also feel bad that they lose out on the joy of remembering good shows, and the lessons that come from recalling the poor ones. The successes keep us coming back, and the lowlights inspire is to keep practicing.

The point is, improv is inherently risky. Sometimes our onstage choices fall flat, or a scene never really finds its feet. The fact that these come more easily to mind can skew your own impression of your success and ability towards the "I suck" side of the scale. But that's not the objective reality, that's just our old friend negativity bias. Remember that the next time you feel like you had a stinker of a show. And next time you have a great show: make a point of savouring that feeling and mentally replaying those highlights. Just to balance things out a little.

But regardless of whether the show was explosively hilarious, or a sneak-out-the-back-without-even-saying-hi-to-your-friends-who-came-to-see-you bomb, you should also bear the following in mind – no matter how it went, you're going to remember the show in a lot more detail, and for a lot longer, than your audience. Because it means a lot more to you than it does to them. In fact, they don't really care that much one way or the other. I mean of course they do, they're your friends. But it's not nearly as important to them as it is to you.

So don't get too low off the lows, nor – for that matter – should you get too high off the highs.

DON'T WORRY, FOCUS OUT

"We never do anything well until we cease to think about the manner of doing it." – William Hazlitt

In one of my first improv workshops, with Keith Johnstone (which was a pretty good place to start), I heard some excellent and oft-repeated advice – make sure your partner is having a good time. That is your job. Your only job.

It's a useful way to frame an improv scene because it takes the pressure off you, allows you to take an attitude of delighted curiosity onto the stage and encourages you to play your scenes with selfless and joyful abandon. That attitude of focusing on your partner and not worrying about your own shit frees you up to just play (to TAKE IT EASY™, if you will).

But there's an important clarification here. You're not *actually* responsible for making sure your partner is having a good time. That's something you can't control. You can only contribute to the possibility of them having a great time by doing things that seem fun – for you and, to the best of your judgement – for your partner. If all is going well, they're doing likewise.

You're in charge of your own good time.

But in actual fact both of you are entirely responsible for your own happiness. So if you're out there giving your all for your partner and they're not giving you much in return, it doesn't matter. If you're bummed out afterward and blame them, I'm sorry to say, that blame is misplaced. You're in charge of your own good time. So if you have a bad show, it's not your partner's fault. It's yours.

Looking after yourself and making sure your partner is having a good time are not mutually exclusive goals. In fact, they support one another. You give, without any need for anything else in return. And that gives you confidence – it frees you up from checking in on your own performance. So you can let go and play.

By focusing outside, you decrease the chances of overthinking.

BOOHOO ON YOUR OWN TIME

"You cannot overestimate the unimportance of practically everything." – Greg McKeown

Let's say you had a real bad show. It probably happens rarely, because you're great. Sometimes, though, it just didn't work. Maybe you personally sucked, or maybe the group collectively dropped the ball, but let's say that *you* particularly and specifically, had a terrible show. You were in your head, you missed some big offers, you hit some bum notes and both the audience and your team seemed less than impressed with you. Whatever.

What can you do? Carry on until the end of the show doing your damned best. Keep going, come what may. My Milly Can Rap counterpart Trent Pancy puts it this way: "We don't celebrate our successes onstage, just as we don't point out our failures." So leave all of those responses until after the show.

Don't sweat your screw-ups. Everyone (except you) will forget about your off-moments either within an hour or a day.

Then when you get offstage, raise your hand and say: "URRHGHGHG! That sucked. I'm an unlovable garbage person. I should quit. Blargh!" Just say it quickly and quietly in the bathroom mirror or out behind the theatre to yourself, and be done with it. If you need to say something to a cast member or your director, do so and be done with it. Spare them the self-flagellation. And especially don't do it in front of an audience member.

Double especially if they thought you had a great show. If they enjoyed it, don't contradict them! Let them have it. And if you suspect they're just being polite by paying you a compliment, just offer a simple "thank you for saying that".

And then... exhale. Shake it off. Let it go. Don't help the negativity bias out by focusing on the negative – the negativity bias will do just fine without your help.

In general, stew a little, shed a lot. Everyone (except you) will forget about your off-moments either within an hour or a day. Because when all's said and done, it isn't about you.

Just do what you can. Let the rest go.

BALANCING THE COMMERCIAL AND ARTISTIC

"Good things happen to those who hustle." – Anaïs Nin

Though it seems to be changing, in my experience paid improv gigs are not the most artistically rewarding occasions for you to perform at. A gig at a company Christmas party or your parents' wedding anniversary, well, there's a good possibility that the set list and content you'll be performing that evening won't be your favourite type of improv.

When I moved to Amsterdam in 2003 and got a job doing corporate shows with Boom Chicago, it was pretty great – at first. And then there were periods when it felt less like I'd achieved something amazing. Sure I was performing improv for a living with top-quality players, while living in Europe, but still, at times, it didn't feel like the pinnacle of my performer dreams.

But then, of course, came the pay cheques to keep me in noodles, Gouda and cheap beer for my year living abroad. In fact, that job was what allowed me to actually make it by that year. And it really sharpened my improv skills. So who cares that the set lists were often similar and I wasn't artistically pushing myself. That wasn't the point.

And it's not just improv – most anytime I get paid for something creative (writing, acting, improv), it's not the purest artistic expression of my craft, but rather a way to put those skills to work for someone else. And for some cash.

But it's always been that way. Filmmakers need to balance their sensibility with what studios want (and what audiences will go see); painters needed to paint portraits of patrons to make that a career; and musicians can develop their craft in secret, but often need to make artistic compromises to reach a wider audience. Not all the time of course, but often enough.

It's the nature of art vs commerce – it's been going on for a long time and is far from something unique to improv.

Definitely find your own voice, do your own thing, but don't turn your nose up at paid work. Or alternately, if you do decline those Christmas parties, corporate teambuilding workshops, or other paid gigs to pursue your own unique artistic vision, that's great. Good on you for the purity of your dedication and so forth. And if you're one of the ones who makes a living for doing their own unique and artistically progressive brand of improv, I congratulate you.

But don't forget everyone has different circumstances and sensibilities, and be careful not to scorn those who make different choices to you. They might have very good reasons for choosing a different path. For instance, they might really need to get paid, or they might just really love teaching Zip Zap Zop to marketing professionals. Whatever it is, let it be.

SKIN IN THE GAME

"Every good painter paints what he is." – Jackson Pollock

The quickest way to get an audience to care is for you yourself to care. If you're invested in what's happening from the start, the audience will pick up on that and be more invested. If you're not, it gives them permission to fold their arms, lean back and shake their heads.

Improv is not a slick and polished art form – even when it's performed at a top-notch level there are some moments when the audience can share in the fact that it's being made up on the fly. It might be genuine surprise on the face of a player, a quirky diversion from the narrative or some good-natured messing with one another. These elements can initially seem like a muddle, but one of improv's greatest assets is the ability to take that ramshackle element or quirk and roll it into the overall piece.

Improv isn't about saying funny things – it's about spontaneously creating a shared reality. It's theatre without a script.

That weird choice you made – to have your character fixated on snow tyres, for example – seemed really tangential and unimportant until the end of the piece when he's able to rescue everyone from the snowbound cabin, say. That tiny detail, which exposed some genuine emotion at the beginning of the show, is seamlessly incorporated and helps the piece achieve a higher level. Basically, it looks great. It looks like good writing.

However, this isn't about whether it looks good or not, this is about whether you're really in this or not. Improv isn't about saying funny things – it's about spontaneously creating a shared reality. It's theatre without a script, and it's often funny, but as a byproduct of the creation process. The more real it is, the better.

Another popular workshop I have is called *Get Real*. Its goal is to help performers get at something that I think is vital – reality. Or authenticity. Some might simply refer to it as 'good acting'. Regardless of what you call it, when it's missing, it's noticeable. A lack of reality (or commitment, or vulnerability) is one of my biggest turn-offs in improv and performance. (And people in general.)

'Real' doesn't mean 'kitchen sink grittiness', nor does it advocate for mundane situations or a lack of character work. 'Real' in this case just means that there needs to be some element of the performer visible and sensible to the audience. There needs to be some 'skin in the game'.

Audiences want to see some aspect of humanity onstage. And the easiest way to show that is by baring a little bit of your soul. Of course, they want that mixed in with talent, experience, passion, polish, wit and lyricism among other things, but they also quite definitely want people who show some measure of who they are.

It's a compelling relationship between the heart and the brain onstage. People want to laugh – they want the performers to be witty and the situations full of humour, but they also want to care about the characters and feel there's some personal investment on the part of the performers. If not, it can still be funny, but it will seldom, if ever, be anything more.

Accounting for taste

When performers attempt to connect with an audience with confidence and consideration they will almost always succeed. Sincerity is a greatly underrated attribute in an improviser.

The ideal default attitude of a player toward their audience is along the lines of: "I'm glad you're here! What I'm about to do (or what I'm doing) is something I'm excited about, I'm proud of, and I want you to like it too. I'm going to enjoy myself up here, and I invite you along for the journey." If any of those sentiments don't apply to the performance you're doing, or the audience you're doing it for, you're in trouble. You want your audience to connect with your characters – whether it's with love, hate, admiration or pity. In fact, it doesn't matter, as long as the people watching care about the characters (and the actors). And that only happens when you start caring.

BE YOURSELF, BE DIFFERENT

"Play well, or play badly, but play truly." – *Constantine Stanislavsky*

In improv, there are roughly two kinds of people – those who drift towards playing characters, and those who more or less perform as themselves.

Of course, quite often when starting, improvisers will be very much themselves onstage, perhaps with a slightly different aspect – like they're a boat captain or married. But over time players tend to move down one of the two paths. Some people gravitate towards characters, and amass and hone a selection of accents, physicalities and so forth. Others naturally settle into playing versions of themselves. I'm the second type. I like playing characters who are very similar to me, only louder.

Character players tend to have big physicalities and a greater vocal range. They can be a stiff-lipped English polo enthusiast in one scene and an inappropriately goofy funeral director in another. The 'self player' may do the same roles in the same scenes, but we see the player much more sharply than the character.

Neither is the 'better' way to improvise, but it's worth your effort to develop in the area you're lacking in. If you're great with characters but rarely play yourself on stage, there's a good chance you're hiding behind your characters and it's impeding your development as an improviser. So give yourself the challenge of stepping out from behind those characters now and again – give yourself more space to be yourself.

On the other hand, if you're always yourself onstage it can be very 'samey' and the risk level is low. It's effective for some stand-up comedians and university lecturers, but in improv we're creating realities from nothing, and if every single reality you create has you as the main character, it gets boring. No offense intended – I know you're a really interesting person – but you need to start making more divergent character choices onstage. You need to build up your character muscle.

Practice this in rehearsal by making small character choices – walk slowly, enter a scene happy, or speak nasally, and keep it for a whole scene. Even a whole show. In addition to being enjoyable for the audience and giving your scene partners more to play with, subtle alterations can give you new insights or angles into the characters you play.

Flexing a greater authenticity and a greater character range will start to pay dividends, especially as they begin to influence one another. You'll find your big characters acquiring more depth and nuance, and the 'self' character developing more variation.

*AIN'T NOTHIN' WRONG
WITH A LITTLE FAILURE*

8

INSPIRATION

LITERAL SHMITERAL

"In my beginnings, is my end." – T.S. Eliot

Inspiration comes in many forms – the suggestion we may take from the audience at the top of the show, the flash of an idea we get while standing on the side or the posture of our scene partner in a certain moment. But it's not where they come from that's most interesting – it's how we use them.

If you're playing a shortform set and get the suggestion of 'printer', for example, the immediate idea might be to use a printing press, or play a student trying to print a term paper, or something that immediately springs to mind when you think of printer.

But what else can you think of that's related to/inspired by printer? A three-year-old learning to write? A counterfeiter making phony hundred-dollar bills? A celebrity caught in a compromising position trying to bargain with the paparazzi? Anything else? Doesn't matter. You only need *one*. A single jumping-off point to inspire your scene. That's not very much at all.

It should come as a relief, but should also feel significant. As Peter Parker's Uncle Ben says: "With great power comes great responsibility." Use that power thoughtfully – the idea you use doesn't need to be the first thing that comes to mind. Your immediate association isn't always the most fruitful direction to go. That might sound contrary to the TAKE IT EASY™ idea, but the fact is when we choose the first thing that comes to mind, we may end up with something that doesn't give us a lot of inspiration.

If this were a business book I might describe that easy direction as 'low-hanging fruit'. As we all know, low-hanging fruit is delicious *and* easy to get at. But to challenge and inspire ourselves (and have a bit more fun), we should push ourselves a little out of the realm of the familiar by inviting some broader associations.

Not only does this give our scenes more room to breathe, but it also gives us the chance to be truly inspired by our suggestions rather than just checking them off.

Things like:

Library = I'm an uptight librarian! Shhhhhhh!

Husband/Wife = We have an unresolved issue!

Factory = I'm putting things on a conveyor belt!

Hotel = We're checking in at the front desk!

I could go on with more of these automatic associations, but I won't.

Hopefully these examples demonstrate that these easy to arrive at associations, while feeling improv-y and fulfilling some of the responsibilities we as performers should feel to 'honour our suggestions', actually start in the same place. At the very beginning, with an almost cliché set-up. Now, it's true that we can go anywhere from that point, and no two scenes will be alike. So that's OK, right?

Not really.

Think about paintings. No two artists paint the same way. But still, if every single one of them painted a bowl of fruit, or a lady with a mysterious smile, it might get a bit boring. Even once we account for all the variations in brushstrokes, colours, materials and so on.

What I'm suggesting is that we vary up the *composition*.

So if the suggestion is factory, the easy (and physically strong) opening is to start putting things on a conveyor belt. But like a painter, you have the power and the responsibility to choose how to compose your scene – to decide what you want to paint. Maybe you want to be in the break room, maybe you're trying to fix the conveyor belt, or you could mime punching in at the clock, and then furtively look over your shoulder before punching in a second time card.

It's not that a conveyor belt is wrong, it's that there's a whole world of options. Let yourself be inspired rather than just grabbing the first thing that pops into your mind.

BEG, BORROW AND STEAL

"You have to steal, steal whatever you see." – Michael Caine

Stand-ups will eviscerate and alienate a joke thief. But improv is different. In improv you're much more free to take ideas because improv isn't so content-driven. Stealing in improv is really about learning from other players and teachers, and informing your own performance with those qualities you admire. I don't condone stealing of anything except hearts, but I do want to encourage experimentation.

The more you let yourself be informed by other players and influenced by what you see, the better you're going to be. In the book *Steal Like An Artist*, Austin Kleon discusses 'good' theft vs 'bad' theft.

Good theft is to honour what you're stealing rather than degrading. It's about studying your theft rather than just skimming it, and stealing from many (i.e. being informed by many works and people you admire, rather than exploiting just one mark). It's also about giving credit. You could argue this undermines the idea that it's stealing. I would argue that while that's true, it actually means you've got more credibility and honour. You also want to transform rather than just imitate, and remix rather than rip off. These last two are, I think, the most crucial.

The more you let yourself be informed by other players and influenced by what you see, the better you're going to be.

Let's say you see a Shakespeare format that uses elements of Shakespeare's comedies (mistaken identity, status reversal) and gets certain ask-fors that are incorporated into the plot, and you just try and do that same thing. Well, rather than making something of your own, you're making a pale imitation.

I'll bet those other people are doing it better, and even if they say that they're cool with you lifting the genre, format, and plot devices they've worked so hard on, they're not. I promise you they're not.

However, let's say you were inspired by that Shakespeare show to look at how they use language, how the character types and thematic tropes drive the story, etc., and use that to inform your own genre show. Maybe it's also a Shakespeare show, but maybe it inspired you to break down a different genre.

Or to use a simpler example – maybe you see a longform show and you like a certain edit they do. You steal that and put it in your show. That's great, it's going to make your existing show more nuanced, more informed. Good stuff. However, if you try and copy their show, that's not cool.

No less an artist than Picasso said: "Bad artists copy, great artists steal." He was making the point that everything has been done before by someone else. Great artists (improvisers) take advantage of this, and allow themselves to be influenced through watching shows, reading books, taking workshops and having late-night festival discussions about forms and styles. Getting informed and influenced is why great writers can also be thought of as great readers. Painters spend time at art galleries and filmmakers watch a lot of movies. Expose yourself to great creators in your field and absorb their lessons.

Quentin Tarantino is a major film fan, and all his movies readily display their influences. And his movies are mostly great – and totally unique. He's taken his love of other directors' work and used it to create a style all his own. Be like him – pick up as much as you can and let it inform your work.

Attribution

If your group does a form or game you saw somewhere else, mention it. If you adopt an exercise from another workshop teacher and use it in your own, share the provenance with the participants. Not only is it the right thing to do, it'll make you look like you've studied a lot. As much as I like to mention it when I made up an exercise, I equally like to come off as considerate and well versed in the work of others.

That's the key. We can all be inspired by others – in fact we *should* be inspired. But rather than doing it verbatim, let it mix with your own creative processes, the personalities and dynamics in your group, and see where you end up.

IMPULSE, INSTINCT AND INTUITION

"There is a voice that doesn't use words. Listen." – Rumi

Spontaneity is at the heart of improvisation. It's what draws us in, and it's what keeps us coming back. But there's more to spontaneity than just 'winging it' – there are different modes of spontaneity and different points of origin. Gaining a more nuanced understanding of how we act when we're not thinking can help us better understand where our ideas and feelings come from. We can use that understanding to develop and improve our spontaneity, that core muscle of improvisation.

Impulse

Impulses originate from our body. When we can't properly explain our reasons for doing something, we say we did it impulsively. Supermarkets put candy and gossipy magazines at the checkout hoping to facilitate an impulse buy from you. It's called an 'impulse buy' because it's not planned – you do it without really thinking about it. That's how you end up with stacks of *People* magazines and more Mars bars than you actually need. (You don't actually ever need any Mars bars. Fact.)

The people who design those supermarkets are masters of understanding how impulses work, and they use this knowledge to influence our purchases. In improv, we seek to understand and utilise impulses for much less cynical reasons.

Impulses take place in the body. Reaching for the pack of spearmint gum without being expressly told by your brain to do so, checking your mobile when you hear it buzz. It operates on the periphery of our awareness. There's no decision to act – it happens in a mental place before decision-making.

And when someone has the impulse to enter a scene, that's the same thing. It's pre-decision. It's not always the right choice, but it's better for you to honour your impulses than to squelch them because then they'll stop coming up at all. You feel it – you do it.

Instinct

Instinct originates in our core. It's what causes migratory animals to travel and cute newborn babies to clutch at your finger. Instinct is honed for survival. When we sharpen our stage instincts, we're teaching ourselves to respond reflexively, without thinking.

Our scene partner might pay our character a compliment, and we instinctively become suspicious. Or our character may push back when being poked one too many times by a belligerent cab driver. Our instincts, like our impulses, aren't always right, but they're useful. They're tied to survival, and even though being onstage isn't actually life-threatening, our instincts will often lead us toward a desired outcome.

Intuition

Intuition is often tied to story sense. An idea like 'I just had a feeling that I should knock at the door in that moment' or 'I knew I should ask her about the soccer game'. When we allow our intuition room to play onstage, it can lead to beautiful spontaneous moments that often have a deeper significance than we might've suspected. In his book *Blink*, Malcolm Gladwell says we know more than we think we do, and we can know things subconsciously, before our conscious mind is aware of them. It happens in the movies when the main character says: "I have a bad feeling about this." And then the hosts of the swanky party grab them and throw them in a dank basement lit only by a bare bulb, and then torture them.

Or, it could be in real life, when things come together. When you were thinking about buying an ice cream, and then you find a five-dollar bill on the ground, so you buy an ice cream. Or when you decide not to skip third-period French class on the day the principal pays a surprise visit. Or any one of those things that seem coincidental or circumstantial, but are actually due to mental processes working below our consciousness.

The power of the three 'i's

Impulse, instinct, and intuition are always working. We can't turn them off, though we can override or ignore them, which happens often enough in real life. Sometimes, in our everyday life, it can be useful to not use these advantages. However, in improv that's rarely the case. It's not uncommon to see a beginner (or even an experienced improviser) freeze up onstage, trying to come up with a 'good' idea. I'd say around 96% of the time, they're not actually trying to come up with an idea; they're trying to override the idea that's in their mind so they can come up with something better.

This means they're in an improv scene trying to tamp down the spontaneous flow to come up with an idea out of their head in the hope it will be better than the idea (or ideas) they already have. This is rarely, if ever, a useful course of action.

You've got all these tools, things that are literally happening in every single moment, as your brain microprocesses what's happening and offers up courses of action. TAKE IT EASY™ and follow those waves. You'll be rewarded.

BE IN THE MOMENT,
NOT YOUR HEAD

9

FUTURE
PROOFING

POSITIVELY POPULAR

"There's only one rule I know of, babies – God damn it, you've got to be kind." – Kurt Vonnegut

Talent will only get you so far. Same with hard work.

How far? Well, all the way to the top potentially. But we can't all be super-talented or else that level of talent would be the norm and thus nothing special. And hard work is, well… *hard*. So the smart among us make an effort to help ourselves out in any way we can, to give ourselves some advantages. One way to help yourself along is to be popular.

Not in the sense of being a shallow people-pleaser, or compromising yourself to add some more friends to your contacts list. But being caring, thoughtful and dependable will help you out in the long run. Not only do you need to be the best damn performer you can be, you need to be as professional as possible with all your commitments, and it helps if you're also not an asshole. It will help you get ahead (this may sound cynical, but if the end result is you being a more helpful team player, then I'd argue that the ends justify the means).

Being caring, thoughtful and dependable will help you out in the long run.

Besides, I'll bet you're already a nice person. You might be an introvert or an extrovert, be brimming with confidence and drive or suffer from cripplingly low self-esteem, but regardless – just do your best to be a decent person in addition to continuing to hone your craft. Go out of your way to do something nice for someone else. If you see a show and really appreciate someone's set, let them know. Be as supportive a player as you can.

I know saying 'be positive' can sound like a whole load of hooey. It's not quite as useless as telling someone who suffers from depression to 'cheer up' (as if they'd never considered that as a possibility), but it seems to sit in the same category.

However, being positive isn't necessarily tied to an emotional state – it's just a way of seeing the world, and it actually affects outcomes. If you can lean in towards a positive perspective, stuff will work out for you.

Not, of course, necessarily in the way you want, but at least in some way. Winners are losers who didn't quit.

I guess the other option is, if you're not loving it, to quit for a while. Maybe forever. The fact is we've only got one life to live, and if you're not getting enough out of something you spend a lot of time doing, like improv, then give it up. Or figure out a way to make it fun for you again.

Being positive isn't necessarily tied to an emotional state – you don't have to be happy to be positive. In fact, by maintaining a glass-half-full perspective, stuff will work out for you. Or at least it will seem to, thanks to your upbeat outlook!

It should be easy to think this way. Improv as an art form thrives on accidents, small breakdowns and little miscommunications or missteps, so when things go sideways in life it can actually be good news, as it's something our improv training has prepared us for[5].

---

5   That may not actually be true, but it's a useful lie we can tell ourselves.

FIVE YEARS FROM NOW

"Comparison is the thief of joy." – Theodore Roosevelt

Life is nasty, brutish and short. It's full of difficulties. People are imperfect and sometimes inscrutable. The best-laid plans go awry and dreams run aground. What was once fun becomes tedious, what was once exhilarating causes heartburn.

So of course, at times, things get frustrating. This happens no matter the pursuit.

In improv, you'll undoubtedly get knocked back, have a run of terrible shows, be part of an interpersonal conflict on your team, get a director who doesn't understand you, nail an audition but not get the part, or any number of a million other little things, and it can get frustrating. It might even make you want to pack it in. Don't.

The easiest way to get some perspective is to ask yourself the big question: 'Will this matter in five years?'

The answer is almost always 'no'.

In five years a poor character choice, a flat moment, a weak show, a blown showcase, a script that didn't turn out as funny as you had hoped, none of it will really matter. In fact, the odds are good you'll be the only one who remembers it. That's how little it means to other people, and also how little it means in the big picture.

The thing that will matter is that you did something you got a lot of joy out of, and didn't get too down over little setbacks. Of course, if you're looking to make improv, or a related pursuit, into a professional thing, well... all the more reason to suck it up and let it go. That little thing doesn't matter – regardless of how huge a deal it seemed in the moment.

That's the way we need to think about it. The fact is that much of life is out of our control. All you can control, in fact, is your own work, and your attitude to it. Besides, you need to fuck up a lot to get to the point where you start making consistent successes. So enjoy those fuck ups – they're getting you in the right direction.

QUIT YOUR DAY JOB (OR DON'T)

"Don't quit your day job." – Some jerk

Improv is a difficult thing to make a living at. Don't take my word for it – just look around your improv community. Most people who make a living at it make a marginal one. They probably don't just perform, they teach classes too, or something connected to improv, like run a theatre. Or they started in improv and still do shows, but now make a living doing something related to improv but which pays better, like writing or acting for TV and film. If they make their money just from performing improv, that's incredible. (And I suspect, with very few exceptions, temporary.)

Before recently cutting down my freelancing activities to accommodate a job as a copywriter at a tech startup, I made a living from teaching and performing improv in Amsterdam and around Europe[6]. It was a tough grind – managing my entrepreneurial admin, organising classes, travelling to festivals, working on forms… At the time I relished the challenge of surviving by my wits and hustle – especially in a foreign country. Some cool gigs came in (giving a workshop to 200 employees of the European Commission in Brussels, going for a week to Corfu with Impro Hotel, building up my own cycle of Level One courses through Mezrab in Amsterdam). It was hard, and uncertain, but it felt

---

6   Also from writing scripts, hosting events, teaching corporate teambuilding workshops (on improv or otherwise), a little bit of voiceover work and teaching writing workshops. All things that relate to improv, or have sprung from it.

good, and also somehow right for me to be a working improviser. Even though I was making a lot of sacrifices.

Eventually I came to the realisation that my single-mindedness was not only limited (and limiting), it was also quite foolhardy. I was exhausted from trying to generate all this improv momentum, and the constant travel was putting a strain on my marriage. Besides, I was getting more and more work as a public-speaking coach, event host and writer.

> Don't ever change. Except when you feel yourself or your circumstances changing. In that case, change.

For me, it just stopped making sense – especially when I could leverage my improv training and writing chops to help me make a decent living in other ways. I still do gigs and teach courses and workshops at festivals, but it's something I do more for fun and as supplementary income. It's taken a lot of the pressure off my improv and allowed me to pursue other areas of work and take on some other projects, like finishing a book.

And so I've been able to adjust my perspective on making a living as an improviser. For me it turned out to not be the be-all end-all I thought it was. Of course, if you can do it, you definitely should. And keep doing it for as long as it works for you. It's fun, surprising and immensely gratifying (in my experience anyway). Don't ever change. Except when you feel yourself or your circumstances changing. In that case, change.

Improv in the background

When you look at performers who you really love, and who are 'successful' (whatever that means to you), recognise that they probably also do other stuff. If they're household names (Will Ferrell, Tina Fey, Amy Poehler) it's because they leveraged those improv skills into success as writers and performers. If they're successful doing other things (self-publishing a book on improv, or whatever), it's because they used their improv to push them into new directions.

As great as improv is in and of itself, it's also an amazing facilitator, lubricant, access point and development tool for a lot of related skills and fields. The ways you can make a living as an improviser seem limited, but the ways to make a living as someone with an improv background are almost unlimited. Because everything you do benefits from your improv training, and some of them pay as well or better than improv.

And if pursuing a living as an improviser isn't for you, there's even better news – improv is a great hobby for those whose professions draw on their improv training very little, if at all (I'm thinking web developers, doctors, geologists and event planners, among others).

Once I opened my mind a little bit, and let in other working opportunities, I was able to leverage my improv background into a varied career that allows me to do shows and teach, but also work on a relatively flexible schedule that has helped me buy a home and bring in regular income. However, it also meant I gave up the idea of myself as this purely artistic spirit. This (quitting your improv dream) may or may not appeal to you. It also may or may not make sense for your circumstances.

But in my case, now that I've managed to live professionally from improv, as well as having taught and performed around Europe and North America, I'm OK with moving into a new phase. Plus, I'm starting to save a little for retirement, and that may be something I'm grateful for down the line.

Don't be shy about expanding your horizons and letting improv be just a part of your practice, or a stepping stone to another career.

SOMETHING FOR THE FELLAS

"An idea built the wall of separation between the sexes, and an idea will crumble it to dust." – Sarah Moore Grimké

Here's a little piece of advice just for the men. Now, I don't mean to mansplain here, but this does bear saying (and repeating) – don't be a sexist asshole.

It might sound easy, and in fact it's quite simple. Unfortunately, in practice it can be challenging. Because as much as we improvisers tend to think of ourselves as a great global community, free of prejudices and negativity, improv is not a place free from sexism, judgements and predatory behaviour. Just like (so it seems) every other industry.

I won't get into what goes on offstage here, but the TAKE IT EASY™ method includes being chill when you're onstage with women[7]. Being an asshole onstage by say, interrupting female players, regularly designating them as secondary character hookers or waitresses, sexually objectifying them, telling them to shut up, or any number of things that might be going on under your awareness, or may (seem to) be rewarded by audience response. Cut it out.

The problem is that this type of behaviour creates a lack of trust, a negative environment, and, consequently, bad improv. So don't be an asshole. Put more positively: be a champ. It's surprising the effect actively being a positive force can have.

For an art form that prides itself on being inclusive and egalitarian, it's astonishing how often women are treated poorly. That can be via exclusion, objectification, actual physical impropriety under

---

7   Or anyone, no matter where they are on the gender spectrum. However, this advice applies most specifically to 'guys' when they're performing with 'girls'.

the guise of 'offers' or any number of other things that might seem funny at the time, but aren't. And certainly aren't funny in retrospect.

When I was growing up, improv was a guy's racket – at least around me. That's not inherently a problem – I loved the camaraderie of practicing and performing with eight or 10 other guys about my age, though I also lamented the lack of women involved. But I get now why it may not have appealed to them.

What woman would want to show up and spend time with a bunch of socially awkward and hyperactive guys in their early twenties who are all trying to one-up each other comedically? Like I said, in my experience I can think of just one or two. Again, there's nothing wrong with improvising with your friends, even if it's all dudes; if your improv group is 15 guys, carry on, my brothers.

Our practice becomes our work.

But as you meet other players, do mixer shows at festivals, or play in mixed jams, a problem can arise. Because those habits you've developed, and those jokes and moves that have gotten laughs from your buddies in a gymnasium without any women around are now internalised. It's now how you play.

So if you've spent a lot of time caricaturing women in your rehearsals, or getting laughs from your friends by trying to get a scene partner (male or female), to give you a blowjob, that will make it into your show. Our practice becomes our work.

At a recent improv festival, which was generally wonderful, I was taken aback by the amount of negativity I saw towards women onstage. Offstage everyone was as wonderful as I hoped they would be. But every night I saw something troubling – a woman objectified, a female performer having her ideas ignored continually by her male castmates, and scenes that included women being murdered (offstage), paid for sex (also offstage), called ugly, and so on. As an audience member it was distracting, as a member of the improv community it was frustrating. Surely we're better than this, I thought. And if we're not, we should be.

And it wasn't just that our play should be more aware socially, for social justice reasons. Because the lesser point (one that is also important) is that it wasn't funny. Treating women onstage as anything less than scene partner geniuses – no matter the dynamic of your group – is amateurish, distracting, unfunny and displays a real lack of sophistication[8].

So, although I try in this book not to be too prescriptive, here I'll tell you this – cut that shit out.

Not because women can't help themselves on their own, or can't 'handle' your bullshit, and not because of systemic oppression, but simply because the work is better as a result.

So be an advocate for equal play, check in with your female counterparts about comfort levels with physical violence and intimacy, but, mostly, you don't need to do anything different. Just come onstage with a warm willingness to play, no matter who your partner is.

---

8   In fact, treating anyone shitty onstage – guy, girl or otherwise – is not cool or funny. It's just gross.

BONUS BIT

SIDECOACH SHOUTS

Sidecoaching is usually done in workshops or classes, where the instructor can feed in directions or points of focus for the onstage participants to consider, while having the opportunity to continue the scene.

SIDECOACH LINE #1: "Look at your partner!" – This basic thing is so key that it's easy to forget. It happens to me too. Often I'll make what I think is a strong character choice and not look at my partner, because I'm looking out the window, or I'm too shy to look up from my shoes. But these are, more often than not, actor issues masquerading as character choices. And when you feel like you're not connected to your scene partner or you're unsure what's happening in the scene, a quick and effective remedy is to make eye contact. It'll immediately connect you to your partner, and that will give them (and you) the information you need for where to go next. Plus it feels good. Connecting more with your partner will clean up a huge chunk of your improv issues.

SIDECOACH LINE #2: "One idea at a time!" – Sometimes when an idea arrives we end up throwing out a whole bunch more ideas related to the first one. This is a type of riffing, and can be a fun and energising game for players and the audience, but just as frequently it means racing past something intriguing to throw out a bunch more one-off gags. For example, say Doctor A mentions that the hospital is experiencing paranormal activity, and Doctor B says: "Yes, there's that elderly Russian lady who haunts cardiology." There might follow a whole bunch more riffs off of this idea (maybe a mysterious creaking in the hallway of the geriatric ward, or a werewolf in the ER, or the demon that haunts the dreams of those in intensive care…).

It could be a lot of fun to build this supernatural hospital world, just by 'Yes, and-ing' that initial offer. It's a fun game, no doubt. But after all of those ideas come a-tumbling out, where do you go next?

Just as easily as riffing on that initial offer, the players could zoom in on what they already have. What's the deal with the old Russian lady ghost? Maybe her name is Olga, and she haunts cardiology because an incompetent surgeon killed her husband. Or perhaps she was a pioneer of open-heart surgery and she died of a heart attack. Who knows? The only way to find out is by exploring. Blasting through associative ideas might be good for a couple of laughs and can even be a fun scene.

It's not that slowing down is necessarily better, it's just that we should always be aware that we can go deeper into one idea, rather than trying to generate more ideas. The best way to do that is to slow down, and focus on what you already have.

SIDECOACH LINE #3: "Not so fast!" – Often people rush through scenes, through lines, through moments. But by slowing down we can let lines land, sit with silence, and allow tension and significance to build. Of course, if we wait too long or wait between every line, the improv seems safe and slow. But if we allow ourselves to be affected by our partners, to let our characters process what they hear, meaning – and drama – accrues.

For example: Son coming in the door: "Dad, I quit my job at shoe store." Dad: "Dammit Kevin, we need that money! Now we're going to lose the house!" That's perfectly fine, good even. But what if we try this? Son coming in the door: "Dad, I quit my job at the shoe store." Dad stops. Looks at his son. Puts paper back up to his face and sighs deeply. Shakes head. Then... Then what?

If he starts yelling, it feels more dangerous. If he says *anything*, it's more powerful, more real than the quick-fire return. And if he doesn't say anything at all? The tension keeps building.

The idea that improv is only fast-talking, funny lines of one-upmanship is far too limited. If we stop and let things affect us, the subsequent action has more depth.

SIDECOACH LINE #4: "Stop talking!" – In every improv class there's someone who talks constantly in scenes. As if they're playing the percentages – "The more I talk, the more likely it is that something good will come out of my mouth." But what actually happens is that everything is diluted; nothing really means anything when it's just a relentless barrage of words. It's such a pleasure to see some variation in line lengths, or improvisers who contribute a great deal to a scene without saying much. I saw a scene where the innocent new hire at an auto repair shop witnessed an unscrupulous scam. As an audience we loved watching that character see this seediness take place, and she didn't even say a word! Even when a character is one of the central players in a scene, they can talk less.

SIDECOACH LINE #5: "Repeat that!" – Sometimes offers get missed, and not only by the person on the receiving end. Sometimes the person giving the offer can say something and miss or undervalue the power in what they're saying. It surprises me how often people make potent beautiful offers that they themselves miss. Of course, a scene partner can always have an emotionally resonant response to something mundane, but that power lies on both sides of the equation. When powerful offers are missed by either side, a scene can fizzle out or meander aimlessly. If you think something important has been missed, repeat it. Or ask for it to be repeated.

SIDECOACH LINE #6: "Make it worse!" – Often in improv (and all the time in real life) we try to control and improve situations. It's something we may have learned when we were younger and our parents were fighting, or at work when an email comes in telling us there's a problem with a project delivery date. Our immediate instinct is to try to improve things. One of the great things about improv is that we don't so much care about problems getting solved. If a character is a germophobe, odds are pretty good that the other player will find some way to leave the windows open, lick spoons or bring home a stray dog. If a high-school science teacher is getting fired, she may end her last class by stealing all the magnesium, or telling all of her students what she really thinks of them, or *something*. I mean, she could just walk out with dignity and hope for a good reference from the principal. But it's probably more fun if she sets the couch in the break room on fire.

SIDECOACH LINE #7: "Go!" – This one I don't often shout at people in a scene. But I have shouted or whispered it to the people standing on the side during a group exercise. I can see their feet moving, or their head turning around as if to say "doesn't anybody else see what this scene needs?" Sure, they were recently in a scene, but the scene in the centre is calling for a lovestruck study partner or a nosy neighbour. You know it, nobody else is going, and your feet are already moving. Go in. Be the thing. Do the part. C'mon!

SIDECOACH LINE #8: "Do the thing!" – Sometimes a simple situation is built up to be something more than it is (a guy worried about proposing, a bank teller not wanting to rob a bank, a politician debating going to war). Yes, sometimes this anxiety and very human reality can be what the scene is about. But sometimes it's just a way to prevent you from stepping into the unknown. And if it is a way to keep you (as a performer) safe, spare us the hand wringing; just fucking do it and let's see what happens.

SIDECOACH LINE #9: "Feel it!" – So often we receive a stimulus and attempt to think our way out of it. We're like, "what would be clever, or what can I say that will 'yes, and' that idea?". These aren't necessarily bad ways to approach it (although we can certainly argue that trying to think up something clever isn't a great way forward), but to focus exclusively on these ways of thinking we leave out something simple and powerful – the emotional response. Not an over-the-top reaction, but some feeling you might have. Maybe your scene partner says: "Well, I don't have rent for you this month." You can think your way through it ("But now I'm going to have to take that promotion at work!"), or access a truthful emotional response – anger, concern, frustration, or disappointment. Take a moment to breathe, and then react emotionally.

SIDECOACH LINE #10:"Speak up!" – Here's a very simple thing you can do to improve your improv: speak louder. There's a reason we make a distinction between a 'whisper' and a 'stage whisper'. It's because a stage whisper is actually quite loud, designed to be heard throughout the entire auditorium, theatre or pub. A real whisper is usually reserved for just one other person. There's a similar distinction between 'talking' and 'talking on stage'. When you're performing, speak loud – louder than you think you need to. Practice with your friends and teammates to make sure you're all projecting (that's the technical term) enough.

I'd say 80% of beginners and a significant percentage of improvisers who have been at it a while could all benefit from speaking up loudly and clearly. (About 10% of the others need to stop shouting all the time. The other 10% are doing just fine, and, not coincidentally, probably have actual theatre training. By the way, taking an acting class is a great idea.)

"Speak up!" (PART 2) – Speaking up is also something you can do offstage. In notes sessions, when something's going on you're not comfortable with, or if you have a great idea, or if you feel like you're being overruled unfairly, let it be known. This is different from being argumentative. Being argumentative means you're not listening to or honouring the other person's point of view. That's not so good. Learn the difference. Instead, make sure you feel you're being respected and respect other people, both onstage and offstage. It's not just about managing negative feelings either – if someone did something great, or you saw something really click, share that appreciation.

FOUR GOOD LINES TO STAY ON TRACK

"Ask the right questions if you're going to find the right answers." – Vanessa Redgrave

If a scene is a forward-moving journey, we can imagine a few different ways the journey can go wrong. Either we stop moving (by freezing up), our scenes start losing momentum, or we start going in the wrong direction.

What I've got here for you are four lines of dialogue that can be dropped into any scene at almost any point and help it stay on the right track and moving. Keep them with you, not as a pre-planning type thing, but as an orientation point.

- "You're right!"
- "That changes everything!"
- "Tell me more!"
- "I know exactly what to do!"

"You're right!"

This exercise helps beginners break down a resistance to their partner's ideas. It's an embodiment of the 'yes' of 'Yes, and', but attributes the idea directly to their partner, empowering them and giving weight to their point of view.

This works for aligning players in terms of content, but can also have a profound effect on the dynamics of a scene. Even if we're not technically blocking our partner, we can sometimes find ourselves playing against our partner's perspective. That can be a fun way to play a scene for some time, but that dynamic will get repetitive. One of the quickest shortcuts for getting out of this pattern is simply two words: you're right.

"That changes everything!"

This is related to the Keith Johnstone game It's Tuesday, where participants find a way to have a big reaction to a mundane piece of information (which in his version is one person saying that it's Tuesday).

It's Tuesday is a good game for practicing this skill of making something – anything – important.

So if someone makes a seemingly throwaway offer like "my car's parked outside", there's always the opportunity to have an It's Tuesday moment and flip the reaction from an 'of course it is' one into an 'OMIGOD! THIS IS A HUGE DEAL!' one.

"That changes everything" automatically invests whatever was just said with major significance. When you say these three words, you don't even need to know why the thing your partner said was important. You can figure that out later.

"Tell me more!"

This is one of the simplest ways to signal that you're listening, and to create space for detail in a scene. If your scene partner tells you something, just ask for more information. It gives them more room to expand on an idea that they had, and if they didn't have much of an idea beyond that initial line, it's even better – it pushes them to expand on what they started.

The subtext of this line is also 'I'm excited about what you're going to say'. Of course your partner's going to be happy to share what's on their mind with that kind of welcome.

I use this phrase a lot in my life outside improv. Often what people say is a mere placeholder for their actual perspective or feelings. A simple "tell me more" gives them the room and some encouragement to better define their worldview. And bring you – and the audience – along.

"I know exactly what to do!"

I learned this from the inimitable improv doyenne Patti Stiles when I sat in on one of her workshops at Impro Hotel in Greece. She had her students set up a complicated scenario, even overfill a scene

with ideas. Then one player would enter the scene with the line
"I know exactly what to do!" and immediately proceed to resolve
whatever the problem was.

I love not only this exercise, but also this "I know exactly what
to do" moment, where a player takes ownership of addressing a
situation instead of treading water, searching for funny lines, or
absolving themselves of responsibility by looking to their partner
for answers. They step in, and confidently start proactively solving
problems. It's delightful to see.

The "I know exactly what to do" attitude isn't actually for walking
into a scene *deus ex machina* and magically fixing everything. In
its simplest form, it just empowers players to forward the action.
This line (and the can-do attitude that supports it) can get a stalled
scene moving again.

*LUCKILY, YOUR SCENE
PARTNER'S A GENIUS*

10

MOVING ON

TOOLS AND TRICKS

Alright, now that you've read the book, you've got the core elements of TAKE IT EASY™ with you. And as you no doubt can see, it's not a specific code or a set of rules, but rather an approach, a way of thinking about improvisation. Do less, be more invested and get more out of it.

These ideas should inform and enhance your play. If you manage to take a bit more time, relax a little, dig in deeper and enjoy it more, there will be faster progress. More fun, less effort and better results.

Taking it easy is just the feeling the flow from one moment to the next. It's this moment. And then this one.

And so on. Enjoy.

11

SOME
GAMES
TO PLAY

WARM-UPS

Zoom

# of players: 4-15

After a few rounds of Zoom the room is always ready for what comes next.

How to play: Zoom is like a lot of other warm-ups (standing in a circle, clapping, passing an impulse) but without the rules even of a Zip Zap Zop. You just look at someone, clap and say "zoom", and they pass it to someone else. People can pass it back and forth, to the person next to them, whatever. It just needs to keep moving.

Teaching notes: It's so damn simple that people often look for something more. There's a tendency for beginners to get bored, and let their mind wander. Or freeze up when they receive the Zoom, or even to try and create something funny because they don't yet trust that their sincere playing of the game is enough. But it is.

The game teaches impulse management – just receive the impulse and pass it along. Do nothing in between (TAKE IT EASY™, if you will). It speeds up and it slows down, people get confused, but these things always work themselves out and nobody ever gets hurt. So already, in the first minutes of the workshop, we're focusing on:

- Making strong offers;
- Full-body listening;
- Accepting mistakes;
- Being in the moment;
- Doing only what is required.

Plus, there's always a story of sorts that comes along in the process of a good round of Zoom – an ebb and flow of events and subtext that's entertaining and has a beginning and an end.

Just as in good scenes, it's a byproduct of being in the moment and going moment by moment. The more we concentrate, the better it gets.

I usually play Zoom first thing in workshops. Once we're out the other side, the group is focused, committed, responsive and ready to rock – warmed up, you could say. Plus it's dead easy to explain and play, and flexible enough to transform into new exercises. What's not to love?

Other Zoom Options

Once a few rounds of Zoom are done, I like to move on to some variations:

Sound Zoom – Same as before only this time only thing you can't say is Zoom. Any other word or sound will do.

Sound Zoom in pairs – Have players break into pairs and play Sound Zoom. This usually escalates quickly, becoming louder and more energetic. Interestingly, it also usually leads to strong relationships and stories tend to emerge organically.

Zoom In The Room – Zoom as usual, only this time moving around the room instead of standing in a circle. This variation especially sharpens focus and rhythm.

Word Cloud Zoom – Coming up with ideas on a theme, or just free-associating on the last thing said. Word Cloud works on free associating, following threads, generating themes and narratives.

Number Zoom – Just choose numbers instead of saying Zoom. When people are really in the flow the numbers are sometimes random, sometimes consecutive, sometimes they're fun math words like 'hypotenuse' and 'integer', then it's back to numbers, then it can be equations. I don't like math, but this exercise is a lot of silly fun.

Absolutely!

# of players: up to 30

The emphasis is on commitment

How to play: The instructor shouts out an activity, phrased as a request (such as "shall we look at this old leather-bound history book we just found?" or "shall we fix this pair of sunglasses?")

Everyone responds with the word "Absolutely!" And then devotes themselves entirely and 'absolutely' to the task.

Teaching notes: While participants are performing the activity the instructor should side coach by asking questions to help the players flesh out their own situations.

If the activity is 'playing the guitar', questions might be: is it an acoustic or electric guitar? Is it yours or is it borrowed? Are you playing at home or somewhere else? Are you by yourself or are people listening. Are you any good? And of course, what song are you playing?

The Yes, Let's connection: There's a classic beginners' warm-up exercise called Yes, Let's!. It's designed to help players be more physical and help create an environment through objects, and thus draw us into the world. The downside of this activity is that it often feels forced. The shouting of "Yes, Let's!" grates on everyone after a while, and it really seems hacky after everyone has played it once.

But I didn't want to lose the positive elements of Yes Let's, so I created this variation.

What It Is/Was/Isn't/Is Specifically

# of players: As many as can move comfortably in the space
The details can always matter more

How to play: The participants roam the roam pointing at objects (not people) and confidently proclaiming what they are – "chair, water bottle, notebook, backpack, door, fire extinguisher…." The goal is to move quickly and not think.

Variations

WHAT IT ISN'T The opposite of the first round. In this round the aim is to roam the room, point at things and say what they are not. People struggle with this much more than you might imagine, because a whole world of possibility is overwhelming. But it's good for expanding the boundaries of what's possible. "Heartworm, glasses, sports practice, Google, laser pointer, mannequin, Ford Motor Company, Albert Einstein, horticulturalist, the Stanley Cup, a shrine." I like this round for the aforementioned ability to expand our circle of references and nouns, and also because it demonstrates to most people that just coming up with random ideas isn't actually easy. And the goal here is, of course, to TAKE IT EASY™.

WHAT IT WAS In this round, the first item you point at, you just say "blank" and the next thing you point at, you say the thing that you had pointed at previously. Let's say the first thing you point at is a chair. "Blank, chair, pair of sneakers, light bulb, doorknob, painting, water bottle." This is usually a struggle for people, as it's a bit of a mind-warp, which is amazing considering it's actually not that difficult, but using our brain to retain information that has just happened causes some difficulties. NOTE: In the set-up, I remind people that if they get stuck or confused, just say "blank" when you point at the next object, and start all over again.

WHAT IT IS SPECIFICALLY If we've played all of these exercises, people will be tired of this game, so I usually vary them up and don't play them all at once, but I think this last round really gets at the heart of how to TAKE IT EASY™. In this round, you point at things and actually describe them, look at them, and become inspired by what you see.

So it might go something like this: "A theatre seat with a ripped corner, a three-quarters empty water bottle with a peeling label, a pair of New Balance sneakers that have spent a lot of time in the mud, a blue Bic ballpoint pen that has no lid…" and so on. What happens in this round is that people realise that checking stuff off a list isn't nearly as rewarding as paying attention to the objects themselves, and working with that. NOTE: I often refer people back to the first round (What it is), which people tire of after about a minute. And I point out how much more sustained the energy is for what it is specifically. The details create momentum and interest, in a way that just rattling off the names of objects can't.

Teaching notes: I often open workshops and class lessons with some combination of these exercises. They're simple, and give a good foundation for how to TAKE IT EASY™. Each one focuses on a slightly different foundational element, and I especially like that they're independent, completely non-threatening and noisy as hell.

Emo Boxes

# of players: 3-5 players per group
Increase the range of expressiveness

How to play: In small groups stand in a circle and get an emotion. The first person in the circle has a mild version of that emotional reaction. As you go round the circle, each subsequent person takes the emotion to a slightly higher state. So if the emotion is anger, the first person would have a mild reaction on low end of the angry scale (something like 'gotten toe stepped on accidentally'). The next person would take a slightly increased level of anger ('cut off on the freeway', perhaps), and the increase continues right on up ('hated high school teacher burns your yearbook', 'cheating ex-boyfriend karate kicks your wedding cake', or 'rude waiter kidnaps a loved one'). It doesn't matter what it is that makes you angry (you don't need to say it), just that the emotion escalates.

Teaching notes: I learned this exercise from Rob Broderick (Abandoman) at a workshop in Brighton. The idea is to build upon the intensity of the emotion that came before, and to find variety in emotional states. Our happiness about getting a text from the girl we're interested in is quite different from the happiness at winning an all-expenses-paid around-the-world trip.

In real life very little we say or do is truly neutral. Nor is it often at the extreme end of the emotional spectrum. Most often we dwell in the nuances. By playing with these emotional states we move from 'emoting' ("I'M AAAAANGRY!!" or "I'M SOOOOO HAPPY!") towards a more surprising and authentic experience, for us, our scene partners and the audience.

MOUTH FIRST

And That's...

# of players: In pairs

In medias res is Latin for 'into the middle of things'. And that's how we start!

How to play: In pairs, one player gives a noun and the other says something immediately thereafter that incorporates that word and begins with "And that's...". The key is that they start speaking as soon as they hear the word, and don't stop until the sentence is done.

Example: 'Pork chop' – "And that's the last time I ever served pork chops!" Then the partners switch roles. 'Hummingbird' – "And that's why a hummingbird's heart doesn't explode!"

This exercise isn't just about learning not to prep or plan – it's also a great way to start an actual scene onstage. Starting with a first line of dialogue such as "And that's where we found the treasure!" or "And that's how I learned I was a terrible mail carrier…" puts your partner – and scene – right in a fun and active beginning. So much possibility!

Teaching notes: I developed this exercise to work the mouth-without-the-brain muscle (so definitely not planning what we're going to say, not even *while* we're speaking).

Too often I see players in shows standing on the side of the stage calculating their next move. Same thing happens in workshops. This isn't bad, but when this is the only way you go at your improv, scenes and moves start to look and feel similar. Besides, that kind of side-of-the-stage planning is more akin to hurriedly writing. Whereas the And That's exercise drills right into a fearless openness that is engaging for an audience and can easily sway into genius[9].

---

9   Every time I've taught this exercise at a festival, a participant has used an "And that's…" moment in the show that evening (see the chapter on 'Practice your practice' for more on moving workshop lessons into shows). It's amazing seeing the shift in energy when someone walks out on stage as if they're finishing a thought. It shakes up the players, the audience and the dynamic of the show. It's not that methodical patient improv isn't a good thing – it definitely is. But honing the ability to launch into something completely unknown is thrilling.

Riff Canoe

# of players: Groups of 2-4

Riding the currents, but paddling in your own direction

How to play: First, get a small group together and get a topic. One player immediately jumps forward and begins riffing on that topic. By 'riff' I mean starts speaking on that topic, but letting themselves be inspired by what's happening and their own associations to move onto other suggested themes and ideas. Whenever another player is inspired by what is happening in the present, they step forward, tag out the other player, and jump into their own riff, inspired by what came before.

There are three main forms a riff can take

Memories – Given a topic, such a 'Switzerland', 'horses' or 'dune buggies', people must come up with a memory or even story they heard, as long as it's real. So 'Switzerland' might inspire a story about the time a Swiss exchange student came to school, or how they used to mix up Sweden and Switzerland, or even a story about Halloween chocolate (inspired by the association between Switzerland and chocolate).

Ideas – This is less tethered to memory, and more to exploring an idea. Using the example of Switzerland above, someone could start "Switzerland is a mountainous country. It seems to me that Swiss people are always frolicking in a field surrounded by snowy peaks, and that really doesn't seem to fit well with the precision of their clocks. Because when you look at the mechanics of a watch, you see so many tiny pieces…." Done well, this should be able to go on almost indefinitely.

Characters – Do either of the above, but in character (see also Character Compilation).

Teaching notes: Riff Canoe is about the flow of ideas and the give and take of focus, as well as connecting ideas and memories. I like to start from authenticity, by doing memories and ideas in sequence. Only when the group has those down do I introduce the idea of doing it in character.

In workshops I've had people present these in groups of three or four and they end up being poetic, comedic, compelling and bittersweet. But of course, the canoe only works when everyone paddles, so the key is to get everyone to contribute. This game works particularly well when players mix up ideas, themes, and characters (although of course characters can reappear).

Chee-yips!

# of players: 4-15

Follow the impulse, change the words

How to play: This is a simple game that helps players spark ideas without being attached to results, and it hinges on a willingness to jump in on others' ideas. In a circle one player begins to say a word, the next player finishes that initial sound with the second part of any word (real or made-up) that uses that beginning.

Example: "Fur…"   "…bucket",   "Craaaaa…"   "…zy", "Suuuuuuh…" "…nnderland"

Besides being fun and silly, Chee-yips encourages players to speak and act without worrying about the next moment. The other role forces players to jump in and support, even if they don't know what their partner's offering.

Solo Chee-yips – Though it sounds (and feels) weird, playing this exercise by yourself is lots of fun. It gets you self-reliant, keeps you mentally nimble and encourages you to skip out of mental patterns at the most elemental level.

Teaching notes: Students feel really weird about this game at first. Which to be honest, I really enjoy. Anyway, once they get the hang of it, it quickly becomes a favourite. People love being liberated from finishing the word, and, on the other side, having someone else do the setup offers an easy finish.

Perpetual Verbal Motion Machine

# of players: 1-3

Learning to let it roll

How to play: Give yourself a word or suggestion as a jumping off point, and just start talking. Vary the emotions, content, volume, and physicality. This is a companion to the Riff Canoe, but with the nonsense turned all the way up.

The content itself isn't important – all that matters is letting the stream of consciousness flow. Something like:

PLAYER 1: Hotdogs are the favourite food of children run through streams of consciousness elemental play organise raindrops throwing stars of punch-drunk elegant waiters....

PLAYER 2: Elegant waiters serve soup in silver pots, which call the kettle black, though they know no bounds beyond the realm of interference which radio harbours the boats steaming ahead, land ho and Lando Calrisssian of the star wars and star jars which fireflies live in....

PLAYER 3: Fireflies camping keep the kindling lit, and moonlight ripples on black water, not causing Iraq any pleasure, but the pain behind the knees causes the boxer to hobble slowly....

Teaching notes: This exercise is a perfect combination of Dadaism, freestyle rapping, extemporaneous pontification and performance art into a kind of non-stop group ramble. As Heraclitus said: "You cannot step into the same river twice, for other waters are continually flowing on." And this is just that: all flow, all change.

It's a great exercise to work the brain-mouth muscle. The more you do it, the easier it gets. Working in pairs or trios keeps the energy fresh and removes the burden of one player needing to sustain the momentum the whole time.

At any point, your partner can jump in and start rambling on their own, using a word or phrase they've just heard to inspire their own ramble. With time it gets easier, and tapping into a flow occurs more readily.

New Clichés

# of players: 3 or 4 players

Because the expression 'dead as a doornail' is, well, dead as a doornail

How to play: One person comes up with a word – a noun works best. The next person uses that word to invent a new expression, like 'pure as open heart surgery', 'quiet as a dinosaur', 'swift as peanut butter', 'happy as a pinball machine', 'one bad tennis racket spoils the whole bunch' and so on. This is pretty fun in itself, but is only half the exercise.

The next step is for the third person to explain why this cliché exists. So they must come up with a justification for why 'quiet as a dinosaur' makes sense ("80% of dinosaurs were herbivores, and moved very slowly"). Or 'pure as open-heart surgery' ("There is no environment more sterile and pure than that of the operating theatre when open-heart surgery is being performed").

Teaching notes: This exercise allows us to work with justifications. (Why not try justifying the expression 'swift as peanut butter[10]' right now?) It also gives us a chance to play around with language and conventions.

---

10 My attempt: Peanut butter production involves the rapid smashing of peanuts, with the bits being poured into hot oil and pushed into jars. It takes about one second to fill a jar.

Most Popular Guy in Town

# of players: 1

Do yourself a favour and take this chance to make a lot of 'wink and finger-gun' gestures

I learned this exercise from San Francisco's Tim Orr. It's a challenging way to get your brain thinking of specifics – character names and details – one after another.

How to play: One player gets up to the front of the room and, while facing downstage centre, 'mime walks' (moves as if walking, but without actually going anywhere) and greets all the 'people' they see by calling out their names and saying something about them.

In the workshop where I learned this exercise, people could go for about 30 seconds – maybe a minute – on first try. I've been working on it since then and I'm now able to get up to about two minutes of stream-of-consciousness names and associations.

Examples

Margo Glass! Great to hear about your apple pie winning the state fair first prize.

Oh, Johnny One-Knife! Congrats on getting your sentence commuted.

Ken Philip Hardman! I heard your house is up for sale, sorry to hear you're moving to Billings, Montana, to start a buffalo farm. We'll miss you!

Liz Young! Well played at the bowling tournament last week.

Hacksaw! Great sound effects on the morning radio show yesterday! I particularly loved that toilet flushing/opera aria mashup. You guys are killing it! Keep it up!

Carly Wunderly! Loved those crab cakes yesterday – thanks, hon!

Brianna Jinterman! Let's go to spin class on Tuesday, yeah? 10am, same as last week?

Teaching notes: The key is to keep the mouth moving. Once we start thinking and rejecting names in favour of other 'better' names, things start falling apart. As a teacher, your main focus is to keep 'the most popular person' churning out names and attributes.

DISCOVERY

Roadshow
# of players: 2

Object as an entry point into everything

How to play: Two players start describing an imaginary object. They can either begin by naming it ("It's an alarm clock") or by giving more general attributes ("It's flat and wooden"). Then the two go together in turns, making the object more and more specific. The players don't do a scene; they just find more details about the object and become more interested in it. It sounds simple, but offers big results. The details (and the objects) become memorable and important.

Teaching notes: This is an amazing exercise for unlocking the power of specificity. In partners, describing and interacting with an imaginary object yields all kinds of information – relationships, personal history, meaning and significance, and story.

Enviro Circle

of players: 4+

Objects create a picture that's worth a thousand words

How to play: This simple exercise is great for groupmind. All you do is get a location and go around the circle adding things to the location. If the suggestion is classroom, it might sound like this: "Chalkboard, desks, globe, windows, principal..." and so on.

For the next round, you'll want to encourage two things:

1. For people to be more specific. This relates to strong ideas. A chalkboard is fine, but what about a chalkboard with a complex mathematical formula on it? Or a chalkboard with the substitute teacher's name written on it? A globe or a dented globe? When we contribute strong specific offers, we start creating a world more rapidly.

2. Encourage people to listen more carefully and to be informed by what others are saying, because rather than just keeping it a generic classroom, we want to build a specific one. So if someone says "a wastebasket full of pumpkin innards" you'll have a different environment than if you had "an empty wastebasket, shiny and transparent"[11].

After a few rounds of this you should start to be able to build fascinating environments through groupmind, and stories will automatically present themselves.

Teaching notes: I love playing this game – with small or big groups, beginners and experienced players. The more experienced players find different things to challenge them in here, but there's plenty of learning for newer improvisers too.

---

11   Keith Johnstone calls this the 'Circle of Expectation'. An idea suggests some possibilities and not some others. To build the world and the story you want to honor these expectations as much as possible.

TRANSFORMATIONS

# of players: 4+

Finding inspiration in body movement, not brain thought

How to play: This deceptively simple exercise is great for getting people out of pre-planning mode and finding inspiration in their body.

Start in a circle. A person mimes an activity with an object (bouncing a basketball or laying a tablecloth on a table, say). The player to their left (or I suppose 'to their right' is also possible) begins to copy the movement with the same object.

And here's where it gets fun. Through their body, the copier allows the movement to become more exploratory. To change, develop and eventually become a new activity with a new object. The trick here is to not have your mind lead (which it will want to do), but to allow the movement to direct you to an unknown place, and let the new object be discovered as a result of that.

An example might be the wrist flick of yo-yoing, gradually becoming some new yo-yo moves and arriving at the ladling of soup out of a large pot into bowls. That soup ladling could then be explored and expanded into, say, fly fishing.

Teaching notes: This exercise is great for helping you trust your body and training you to leave the brain outside of the process at times. When the transformation is taking place organically, it's absolutely riveting to watch – provided the head isn't cheating us out of the process.

I like to explain that those moments of not knowing, of discovery, are thrilling for players and audiences, and are actually the essence of improv. Don't cheat yourself or the audience out of those moments.

Character Compilation

# of players: 3+

Many people means many perspectives

How to play: Based on a chosen topic (like camping, dental hygiene, algebra, national parks, memory...) someone steps forward and begins a character-driven monologue or solo scene, utilising that character's unique perspective – either on that general topic, a specific event in that category or a related topic.

For example, if the topic is camping, it could be:

- A father who loves camping with the family;
- A girl who wishes she was at Sally Henderson's party rather than stupid camping with her stupid family;
- An old Boy Scout leader who knows every camping hack there is;
- A barista who thinks camping is a pathetic attempt to relive primitive conditions;
- A campsite owner who can't face another summer of idiots in tents;
- A hermit who lives in the woods and accepts no form of government;
- An 18th-century fur trader, checking his traps on the north face of the Laurentian Shield.

Any topic becomes a launching point for a smorgasbord of characters – perhaps related to each other, perhaps not. All that's required is that they have their own perspective.

Teaching notes: This is great for giving players an opportunity to play in character, explore topics and start finding and creating links that will help them make better organic longform.

CONNECTIONS

Pattern Circle

# of players: 5+

Sounds like an arts-and-crafts project, and, in a way, it is

How to play: I learned this exercise from Trent Pancy in Finland. It helps participants get used to associating with one another's ideas. From one word, the group just associates, as many rounds as required, to get back to that original word.

So for example it might go: car, hubcap, wheel, fortune, game show, contestant, buzzer, delivery, pizza, Mozzarella, Gouda, Cheddar, money, wallet, billfold, purse, prize, lottery, scratch, ticket, bingo, blackout, drunk, hangover, brunch, Bloody Mary, Eggs Benedict, waiter, kitchen, order, soldiers, trench, enemy, victory, lap, race, car.

Teaching notes: The key is to associate on the word you just heard but to keep in mind the other words that came before to build one-to-one connections, larger patterns, collections of patterns, all with the goal of getting back to the original word. Any forcing of ideas or a return to the original word will be jarring. But once the flow is in place, a return becomes almost inevitable, and immensely satisfying.

I'm a Tree

# of players: 3

The beautiful rule of three

How to play: All three participants create a scenario collaboratively.

- I'm a tree.
- I'm a bird in the tree.
- I'm a path leading to the tree.

Or

- I'm a spaceship.
- I'm a spaceman.
- I'm the moon.

Every subsequent tableau comes from whoever is in position one taking one of the other two out of the centre, leaving the third in the middle. The player then restates their offer, and becomes the foundation for the next tableau.

In the example above, Spaceship may 'take' Spaceman, leaving moon. Then the next tableau may go

- I'm the moon.
- I'm a telescope.
- I'm a moon rock.

And so on.

Teaching notes: This is a great exercise for beginners, getting them contributing and feeling free to share their associations. We want every set of three to be connected, though the newest iteration of the game is the one we want to focus on. But for groups that don't know this exercise, this above 'tableaux' version is enough.

I'm a Tree: Part 2

How to play: Same as the above version, but in this case the workshop leader needs to be critical, making sure all three elements are connected, and insisting that each new offer relates to each element that came before. For example:

- I'm a tennis player.
- I'm her incredible backhand stroke.
- I'm the scar tissue growing in the tendons of her elbow.

Tennis player and backhand stroke are connected, so that's easy. But what if the third offer were "I'm a tennis ball" or "I'm the ball boy on the sidelines"? Yes, they fit the setting, and therefore *seem* appropriate. But they don't elaborate on or heighten the ideas that have come before.

To make this game really work effectively, we want the second offer to connect to the first, and add more specificity. The third idea connects to *both* one and two. By doing so it offers a completion of the idea that came before – we get a sort of 'narrative closure'.

More examples:
- I'm a murder of crows.
- I'm a scarecrow.
- I'm a satisfied farmer watching those crows fly away.

- I'm a farmer.
- I'm the farmer's brand new tractor.
- I'm a jealous neighbour.

- I'm a neighbour.
- I'm a new family moving in.
- I'm the telescope used to spy on the new family.

- I'm a telescope.
- I'm an astronomer discovering a new planet.
- I'm the woman he named that planet after.

Sometimes the connection of ideas will generate a laugh, and other times they'll just feel satisfying. The point is to simply keep training yourself to make connections between all the preceding elements.

This way you'll start moving away from point-to-point-to-point single-layer narratives, towards unified stories that incorporate all the info that comes before.

Teaching notes: I learned this enhanced version of I'm A Tree from Stephen Sim of Winnipeg, and have found it an invaluable way of teaching people to connect ideas and serve the story. In fact, it's one of the single best ways to get people to really understand what the process of improvising should look and feel like.

One easy way to see if this exercise is working is by seeing how the group responds to each set of three. Laughter after the third offer is a good sign that the connection was sharp. But sometimes it can be a silence or gasp. Basically, when the set of three is strong, the energy in the room responds.

We can also recognise the power and utility of specificity. This is not about making things more complicated or being long-winded, it's really about making the ideas specific and taking connections that might be implied (or even 'weak'), and making them firm and evocative.

Mind Meld

# of players: 5+

Communal conjunction is the function

Mind Meld (also called Confluence, Convergence or 3,2,1 Contact) is a satisfying experience of going from diversity to connection. I first learned this from Nicole Mischler in Amsterdam, and found it an excellent exercise for strenghtening connectivity.

How to play: Everyone in the circle thinks of a word. The first person to have a word in mind says "One!", the second says "Two!". They run into the centre and say "Three!" together, then call out their words at the same time. For example: 'belt' and 'sports car'.

They rejoin the circle, and everyone else looks for a connection between the two words, the first person to have one calls out "One!", the second says "Two!". They go into the centre, say

"Three!" together and call out their words. (In this case, maybe 'engine' and 'dress shirt').

The round is over when the two people in the middle shout out the same word.

Teaching notes: There's no need to explain connections, second-guess or discuss. The two just rejoin the circle. And as they go back to the circle everyone looks for a new connection between the two most recent words (in this case, possibly 'stain' and 'mechanic'. Repeat.

Count to 20

# of players: 4-20

Moving on up, in a connected way

This is a classic improv warm-up, and is great for getting people to feel connected. It also has a mildly meditative quality.

How to play: Simply have the group stand in a circle and count from one to 20, without going in a pattern and without providing any clues as to who's going to speak next. Each player can say one number per turn. If two players start to say a number at the same time, begin back at one.

Teaching notes: If things aren't going well (the group keeps getting stuck), frustration sets in, but a frustrated group will never succeed. It's only by pushing past the frustration and relaxing back into the exercise that a group will be able to complete the task.

Do it with your eyes closed or while walking around the space. It may take you a few (or many) attempts to get to 20, but if you TAKE IT EASY™ you'll get there.

SCENES AND SCENEWORK

That Makes Me Feel...

# of players: 2

Emotional impact over everything else

I first learned this exercise from its creators, Marshall Stern and Nancy Howland Walker of Zenprov. It's an excellent exercise for not only *really* listening to your partner and yourself – it's also a shortcut to getting to an emotional space without worrying about content.

How to play: Two players get up as if to perform a scene. However, rather than performing a two-person scene, they stand facing one another and honestly respond to one another.

The first line is: "I feel_____". The partner responds with "That makes me feel _____" and they go back and forth, being changed by what their partner has said.

The 'scene' will either find a natural conclusion or the workshop facilitator can call it when they feel it's reached a natural close.

Teaching notes: If one or more players aren't fully committed, or they're having a feeling and not giving voice to it, this exercise is maddening. Unless their partner addresses that disconnect, in which case this exercise becomes really interesting

If played well (that is sincerely, by two players responding in the moment to what their partner has given them) this exercise is riveting – even jaw-dropping. It's a strong demonstration, to those playing and those watching, what improvised theatre can do when players are honest with themselves, their partner and the audience. Vulnerability and authenticity can be a show of strength.

Meisner

# of players: 2

Getting through the content, directly to the noticing

This is an adaptation of Sanford Meisner's revolutionary repetition exercise for actors. I don't remember where I first played it in an improv context, but I originally studied the Meisner technique during my acting training, and found it transformative. Applied to improv, it's just as powerful.

How to play: The improvisers get into pairs and stand facing one another and just comment on what they see. The partner just responds affirming what the first player has said (even if they don't agree). The players repeat back and forth until one player is inspired to change the phrase. When that happens, the new phrase is repeated back and forth, perhaps being altered slightly, until a new observation presents itself.

Example

The first round might be:

Player 1: You've got brown hair.

Player 2: I've got brown hair.

Player 1: You've got brown hair.

Player 2: I've got brown hair.

Player 1: You're scratching your nose.

Player 2: I'm scratching my nose.

And on and on with the back-and-forth. The idea is to get the players to focus outwards and notice their scene partner and what they're doing. Even though this is a very unnatural way to have a conversation, with practice it will start to feel natural, and players can enter an almost trance-like state.

The next stage is to have players make observations about the emotional state of their partner.

Example:

Player 1: You're bored.

Player 2: I'm bored.

Player 1: You're bored.

Player 2: I'm bored.

Player 1: You're bored.

Player 2: You're accusing me.

Player 1: I'm accusing you?

Player 2: Yeah, you're accusing me.

Player 1: You feel guilty!

Teaching note: It's important in the repetition that players don't reject what their partner says, instead they just accept and work with what they hear (it's like improv that way). So there's no rejecting of observations.

Once you've been training in this for a while, you'll be able to use it to stay focused on your scene partner and be present in the moment by commenting on activities you witness.

Now we do repetition, so in pairs each person looks at their partner and comments (in a non-judgemental way) on them. The other person responds, so there's a back-and-forth flow of observation and acceptance. E.g. "You have brown hair" "I have brown hair" "You have brown hair" "You're looking at me" "I'm looking at you"

The next step is to have people notice and make assumptions. E.g. "You're angry" "I'm angry"

The third step is to make assumptions and have the partner make justifications. Like, "You look happy!" "I just won the lottery!"

NOTE: It's also acceptable to make justifications inspired by the other person's expression. E.g. "You look like you just got fired." In fact, this can even be a later round.

Scenes 1-30

# of players: 2

Let the connection do the work

The first time I had workshop participants play this exercise, I wasn't quite sure what to expect. But what I saw was some brilliantly nuanced, completely detailed and enthralling scenes with complete and clear stories between two grounded characters. When we don't have words to carry our meaning, we become more expressive, using the other tools – our faces, bodies, eye contact and tone.

How to play: Two players perform an honest emotionally driven scene where the only dialogue is the numbers in order, from one to 30.

Teaching notes: So much information can be conveyed between actors and from stage to audience without dialogue. And if we add dialogue it would be even more intense. In fact, these scenes with no dialogue were already emotionally turbocharged and had the capacity to move the audience.

Out of Body

# of players: 2

A scenic walk-through; going through the motions

I learned this from Jacob Banigan of Austria. It sharpens storytelling, but unlike other storytelling games, manages to keep players engaged with being 'in' the story.

How to play: In this exercise you get participants to talk through rather than act out scenes. Rather than being 'in' the scenes, the players 'work' through them collaboratively.

If a suggestion for a scene between two players were 'beekeeper', it might play out like this:

Player 1: I come on as a beekeeper, tending to my hives.

Player 2: I'm the beekeeper's apprentice, and I show up, yawning.

Player 1: I comment on the apprentice's late arrival, and warn her that next time she's late, she'll be fired.

Player 2: I explain that I've been moonlighting as an exterminator.

Player 1: I express outrage that anyone would kill such majestic creatures as insects.

A third person jumps up, sensing an opportunity to contribute

Player 3: I'm a third person, a neighbour, coming over to get some sweet, sweet honey.

Player 2: I point to my boss that we have a customer.

Player 1: I greet my neighbour with a big exaggerated wave and smile.

And so on.

Teaching notes: Players should only ever be contributing what they or their characters are able to provide (they should not be giving directions or demanding their scene partner do something). The strength of this exercise is in providing an overall approach by seeing the mechanics of a scene beat-by-beat. Working it out this way helps heighten players' awareness of the overall direction in story.

It doesn't sharpen players' instinctual approach to improv, or help them delve into characters, but what it does do – by removing the responsibility of acting and developing character – can be a powerful catalyst for players who may get stuck in scenes. Or for those who are keen to bring in 'wacky' offers – they really stick out during this exercise.

FINAL WORD

I hope you enjoyed the book, and will take some of the ideas, insights and exercises into your own improv practice. I'll leave the last word to ancient Chinese philosopher Lao Tzu, the founder of Taoism:

"When the student is ready the teacher will appear. When the student is truly ready, the teacher will disappear." – Lao Tzu.

Poof!

SUPPORTERS

Many big thanks to these wonderful people for their generous support of this book project.

Charles Loui-Ying, Jules Munns, Mary O'Mahony, Lew Dumontet, Nickie Lennon, Bob Makarowski, Ando Roots, Matthew Fishwick, Patrick Boylan, Mirko Fichtner, Anne Maycock, Marcy Keehn, Selina Chiarelli, Alastair Thomas, Sarah Rose, Dom Gittins, Lisa Knelange, Sam Super, Darren Millar, Neil Morgan, Bruce Seymour, Robin Straaijer, Anja Sophie Boorsma, Rory Brosnan, Kyla Bruce, Hongji Liu, Paolo Busi, Janne Lesonen, Juho Fröjd, Willem van Strien, Katy Schutte, Shayne Smart, Uri Lifshitz, Percy Brosnan, Cale Bain, Lindsey Richardson, Megan Millar, Geoff & Helen Millar, Ian & Linna Morgan, Chris Nelisse, Ben Verhoeven, Dave Morris, Noah Levin, Henrik Esperi

Thank you all!

PATRONS

Enormous thank yous to these wonderful folks for their above-and-beyond assistance in the production of this book. You guys rock!

Derek Morgan, Glynne Steele, Dave Sawyer, Mika Kemppi, Conrad Toft, Paul Turner, Kendra Morgan, Jim Libby, Kiki Hohnen, Ryan Cofrancesco, Geordie Aitken, Leigh Morgan, Cameron McLeod, John Handscombe.

Big hugs and a huge round of applause for them please!

And thanks of course to you for reading!

Goodnight!

POSTSCRIPT

Keep in touch! If you enjoyed this book join my mailing list at www.ryanmillar.com for irregular news and updates and more great reading.

EVERY ENDING IS THE START OF SOMETHING ELSE